W9-ADO-021

Special Education

What It Is and Why We Need It

Special Education

What It Is and Why We Need It

James M. Kauffman
University of Virginia

Daniel P. Hallahan
University of Virginia

Boston   New York   San Francisco
Mexico City   Montreal   Toronto   London   Madrid   Munich   Paris
Hong Kong   Singapore   Tokyo   Cape Town   Sydney

Executive Editor: *Virginia Lanigan*
Series Editorial Assistant: *Scott Blaszak*
Executive Marketing Manager: *Amy Cronin-Jordan*
Senior Production Editor: *Annette Pagliaro*
Composition Buyer: *Linda Cox*
Manufacturing Buyer: *Andrew Turso*
Cover Administrator: *Rebecca Krzyzaniak*
Text Composition: *Omegatype Typography, Inc.*

For related titles and support materials, visit our online catalog at www.ablongman.com.

Copyright © 2005 Pearson Education, Inc.

All rights reserved. No part of the material protected by this copyright notice may be repro-duced or utilized in any form or by any means, electronic or mechanical, including photocopy-ing, recording, or by any information storage and retrieval system, without written permission from the copyright owner.

To obtain permission(s) to use material from this work, please submit a written request to Allyn and Bacon, Permissions Department, 75 Arlington Street, Boston, MA 02116 or fax your request to 617-848-7320.

Between the time Website information is gathered and then published, it is not unusual for some sites to have closed. Also, the transcription of URLs can result in unintended typograph-ical errors. The publisher would appreciate notification where these errors occur so that they may be corrected in subsequent editions.

Library of Congress Cataloging-in-Publication Data

Kauffman, James M.
    Special education : what it is and why we need it / James M. Kauffman, Daniel P. Hallahan.
    p.   cm.
    Includes bibliographical references and index.
    ISBN 0-205-42039-7 (alk. paper)
        1. Special education—United States.   I. Hallahan, Daniel P., 1944–   II. Title.

LC3981.K38 2005
371.9'0973—dc22

2004053365

Printed in the United States of America
10   9   8   7   08

CONTENTS

Preface   vii

1 The Puzzle of Special Education   1

Common Misconceptions   1
Brief History of Special Education in the United States   3
Contemporary and Perpetual Issues   7
Questions in the Puzzle and Nature of the Dilemma   8
Summary   10
Box 1.1: Case in Point   10
Reference Notes   11

2 Measurement of Educational Performance   12

The Problem of Measurement in Education   12
What Is a Statistical Distribution?   18
How Can and Should Special Education Change Performance?   24
Summary   26
Box 2.1: Case in Point   26
Reference Notes   26

3 The Nature of Educational Disabilities   28

Three Important Points About Disabilities and Exceptionalities   30
Mental Retardation   31
Learning Disability   33
Attention Deficit-Hyperactivity Disorder   34
Emotional or Behavioral Disorder   35
Communication Disorder   36
Deafness   37
Vision Impairment and Blindness   38

Physical Disability   39

Autistic Spectrum Disorder   40

Traumatic Brain Injury   40

Deaf-Blindness and Other Severe and Multiple Disabilities   41

Giftedness and Special Talents   42

Why Prevention of Disabilities Is Often Not Practiced   43

Summary   45

Box 3.1: Case in Point   45

Reference Notes   46

4 **The Nature of Special Education**   47

How Special Education Is—or Can Be—Special   47

Special Education on a Continuum   53

Special Education's Bottom Line   54

Summary   55

Box 4.1: Case in Point   55

Reference Notes   56

5 **Frequent Criticisms and Responses to Them**   57

Responses to Criticisms   57

Other Questions About Special Education   64

Summary   72

Box 5.1: Case in Point   72

Reference Notes   73

References   75

Index   81

PREFACE

The *idea* of special education is entirely justifiable. The concept is not merely sound but essential to universal education in a democratic and benevolent society. Special education is a powerful concept, which leaves it open to strong opinions in support and in opposition. And it is a complex practice, which sometimes results in it being practiced poorly, and, in many instances, superbly. Our intention is to help readers understand both the integrity of the concept of special education and the characteristics of good practices.

Intended Audiences and Uses

This booklet is not intended as a "stand-alone" text for an introductory course in special education. It is intended as a supplement in which only the most basic problems and features of special education are introduced. We see it as a convenient summary of basic ideas that may be used as a supplement for a beginning course in special education, an informative supplement to a general education course in which some working knowledge of special education concepts is important, or a basic explanation to parents of children who are curious about what special education is and what it should be. We realize that we do not address all issues in sufficient detail to satisfy all readers or deal with any issue in the depth that some readers may expect.

In our first chapter, we discuss some general concepts of universal public education and special education to set the stage for discussion to follow. Universal public education inevitably brings us to a puzzle that can be solved only by introducing the concept of special education. Without special education, the puzzle cannot be solved, and we explain why this is so.

In our second chapter we take up the topic of measurement of human performance, which is an integral part of general and special education. We explain why understanding measurement, including the distribution of performance that measurement unfailingly produces, is at the heart of special education. Understanding special education is possible only if one understands the nature of measurement and statistical distributions.

In Chapter 3 we discuss the nature of disabilities. We define and describe the types of disabilities that typically require special education. Without an understanding of the basis for these categories of disability, one simply cannot understand what special education is designed to do. True, the individual needs of students must be described, but in describing them we inevitably describe categories of need. Categories are as unavoidable as the differences they describe.

Chapter 4 is our attempt to describe special education in unmistakable terms. Too often the role of special education has been portrayed in unflattering ways or has been misrepresented. We describe what it should be and can be when it is practiced well and what distinguishes it from general education.

In Chapter 5 we take up criticisms of special education that we have frequently encountered, and suggest reasoned responses to them. In many ways these are perpetual issues—controversies that are at the center of thinking about special education—and many of them will never, in our opinion, be entirely resolved in a democratic society. If by the time you read Chapter 5 you think you can answer the criticisms yourself based on your reading of the previous chapters, then you are to be congratulated.

Acknowledgments

We are particularly grateful to Virginia Lanigan, our editor at Allyn & Bacon, for her support of this project and her fine editorial suggestions. We thank our reviewers: Tunjarnika L. Coleman-Ferrell, Palm Beach community college; Elizabeth Cramer, Florida International University; Carl L. Ferguson, Jr., Armstrong Atlantic State University; David Forbush, Utah State University; Jackie Paxton, University of Arkansas–Fort Smith; and Cynthia Herr, University of Oregon. We are grateful to Devery R. Mock, University of Iowa, for her assistance in searching the literature. Finally, both of us must acknowledge the influence of our mentors on our thinking about special education, Richard J. Whelan (for JMK at the University of Kansas) and the late William M. Cruickshank (for DPH at the University of Michigan).

James M. Kauffman
Daniel P. Hallahan
Charlottesville, Virginia

Special Education

What It Is and Why We Need It

1 The Puzzle of Special Education

"Special education" is a term often used in schooling today. However, misunderstanding of special education is common, even among educators. Just *what* special education *is, who* gets it or who *should* get it, and *why* it is necessary are matters that relatively few teachers, parents, school administrators, or educators of teachers can explain accurately or with much confidence.

Our intention is to help you build a foundation of understanding, to begin at the beginning and fashion a realistic, rational view of the basic assumptions and knowledge on which special education rests. Only after doing this can any of us sort through the various statements that we read and hear about special education and separate the facts from misinformation. Only then can we reasonably consider any proposals for change or reform.

After reading this booklet, you should be able to explain what special education is (and what it is not), how it differs from general education, why we need it, and what we might expect as reasonable outcomes for students if special education is what it should be. It should give you a sound basis for separating facts from misconceptions about some of the central ideas in special education.

Special education is a puzzle that is not easily solved. We begin this chapter by describing misconceptions about this puzzle and correct them with statements that are more accurate. Then we sketch the history of special education in the United States. We explain why the puzzle exists and touch on dilemmas that will always exist in education—the perpetual issues.

Common Misconceptions

Misconception and misunderstanding of special education are common. Following are some of the most common misconceptions we have heard, along with more accurate statements of fact.[1]

- *Misconception:* Special education is just good education—good teaching of the kind that every student should have. There is nothing really *special* about it.

1

- *Fact:* Special education is not just good education for typical students but instruction that differs significantly from what is effective for typical students—special in ways we will discuss in a later chapter.
- *Misconception:* Special education is mainly a matter of having patience, of being tolerant of students who don't learn readily or behave well.
- *Fact:* Teaching anything well requires patience with learners, but far more than patience and tolerance is required in special education. Precision and explicitness are probably at least as important as patience in special education.
- *Misconception:* Kids who need special education are mentally retarded.
- *Fact:* Most students with mental retardation do need special education, but mental retardation is not the most common disability requiring special education. Further, most of the students receiving special education are not mentally retarded.
- *Misconception:* Special education is where they put kids who are problems or don't fit in, just to get rid of them.
- *Fact:* Many students receiving special education do not receive it because they are perceived as *being* problems but because they are seen as *having* problems in learning. Furthermore, special education is never legitimately—and is not usually—just a way for a teacher to get rid of a problem.
- *Misconception:* Special education is like a roach motel: You go in, but you don't come out. The fact that so few children exit special education is scandalous.
- *Fact:* No one knows how to cure most disabilities; most children with disabilities will require special education throughout their school years if they are to make reasonable progress. They have *developmental* disabilities for which no cure is known. The fact that a relatively small number of students receiving special education are eventually found not to need it does not mean that their special education has been ineffective.
- *Misconception:* Special education prevents students from achieving at a higher level because it offers only a watered-down curriculum and low expectations.
- *Fact:* Special education should, and often does, help students learn more than they would otherwise. Many students do need a curriculum that is different from that appropriate for typical students
- *Misconception:* Special education is discriminatory and segregationist—it serves mostly ethnic minority kids and shunts them into dead-end special classes where they squander their time.
- *Fact:* Most of the students receiving special education are Caucasian (about 3.5 million of about 5.5 million children, or about 63% of all children with disabilities receiving special education, according to the National Research Council report of 2002).[2] However, a disproportionately large or a disproportionately small number of children from some ethnic groups receives special education, particularly in some categories. This fact may have as much to do with the experiences of these children outside of school as it does with unfair treatment in school. Furthermore, special education is not necessarily a "dead end." General

education is and always will be a "dead end" for *some* students if their educational needs are not identified and served appropriately.

- *Misconception:* Special education is required for all children with disabilities because kids with disabilities simply can't be expected to learn much.
- *Fact:* Some students with disabilities do just fine in general education and do not require special education. Others will fail in the general curriculum by any reasonable standard. However, special education's purpose is helping students with disabilities learn all they can in school, and for most students with disabilities this means learning a lot.
- *Misconception:* Special education is basically unfair, because some kids get educational opportunities or have special protections that other kids don't.
- *Fact:* Fairness does not mean treating all students exactly the same regardless of their abilities. Some students have disabilities that require education that is different from the typical if they are to be treated fairly. Without special protections, the atypical students who need special education will not get fair treatment. Fairness in education means that every child receives the instruction that he or she needs, even if it is different from what most children need.
- *Misconception:* Special education wouldn't be needed at all if general (regular) education did its job well.
- *Fact:* Regular or general education has to be designed for the student who falls within a range of "typical" or "normal" development. Even if teachers are doing a superb job they cannot prevent all disabilities or provide the instruction that all students with disabilities (i.e., the markedly atypical students) need.

Hearing only the misconceptions about special education might lead us to believe that it is an ineffective, misguided, and even harmful set of practices. Although special education has often been badly practiced and suffered abuses, it is an idea and a set of recommended practices that can make (and often has made) public schooling fairer and more effective than it would otherwise be. Historically, it represents the intention to make sure that students with disabilities are not neglected, that they learn all they can, and that they are given a fair shake in school.

Brief History of Special Education in the United States

Special education has its roots in European history, particularly the era of the French Revolution and the Enlightenment, when egalitarianism, reason, and science became dominant social forces.[3] In the United States, the first formal attempts to provide special education date from the 19th century, when special schools were set up for children who were blind or deaf (or both) or mentally retarded. Before these special schools were established, children with disabilities were cared for at home and usually were offered nothing at all in the way of formal education, unless their family could pay the cost of private and highly unusual education. Special schools played a very significant part in the early days of special education. The "universal" public schooling beginning in the mid-1800s did not include schooling for children with disabilities.

In the late 19th century, large metropolitan school districts, such as New York City Public Schools, were faced with several problems: large numbers of immigrant children who spoke little or no English; large numbers of truant, "wayward," and delinquent youths; and substantial numbers of children who spoke English but could not learn the standard curriculum of the schools with typical teaching procedures. Faced with these problems of the late 19th and early 20th centuries, some large metropolitan school districts instituted special classes. Some of these classes were for "steamer children," recent immigrants who were learning English. (Today, we call them English Language Learners [ELL] or students of English as a Second Language [ESL].) Other special classes were for truant and delinquent students, many of whom today would probably be called emotionally disturbed. Still others were for "laggards" or "slow" children whose rate of learning was markedly slower than the typical student. (Today, we would probably say that they have mild mental retardation or learning disabilities.) In many special classes, there was a strong emphasis on vocational skills and work habits in addition to very basic academics.

At the same time, large metropolitan school districts also found students whose rate of learning was extraordinarily high. Special classes and schools for these very high achievers, who today might be called gifted or talented, allowed them to proceed at a high rate of learning and to reach very advanced levels of performance, often in specific areas such as science or the arts.

In short, a major problem of large city school districts at the beginning of the 20th century was extreme variability among the children to be taught in systems that required school attendance. The solution to the problem was special education in the form of special classes and schools offering a wide variety of curricula and methods of teaching. In many ways, the problem of universal public education remains the same today, and in some respects a better solution has not been found. Judy Singer wrote in 1988, "Special education was the solution to the regular educator's thorny problem of how to provide supplemental resources to children in need while not shortchanging other students in the class. Nothing else has happened within regular education to solve this problem."[4]

By the 1920s, most school districts in the United States had mandatory attendance laws and attempted to accommodate a wide variety of students. This was the era in which special education became commonplace in large cities and professional associations such as the Council for Exceptional Children were founded. After World War II, special education became more common in smaller school systems, due in large part to the action of parents in pressing schools for special services through parent organizations such as the National Association for Retarded Children (later called the Association for Retarded Citizens and now known simply as The ARC).[5]

The 1960s saw the first federal legislation involving special education. By the mid-1960s, federal laws had established a federal Bureau of Education for the Handicapped (BEH) in the Office of Education (now the Office of Special Education Programs, or OSEP, in the U.S. Department of Education). The Bureau (BEH) offered grants to states, college, and universities. These grants supported special education through the establishment of state agencies and resource centers offering special materials and consultation to schools. Prominent features of federal grants in this era were teacher training and advanced graduate training for those who were to prepare special teachers for students with disabilities (then called "handicapped children"). Many thousands of teachers and many hundreds of teacher educators were trained with federal assistance in the 1960s. In fact, a presidential commission on mental retardation set as a goal training 70,000 teachers of students with mental retardation by the end of the 1960s.

Although special education expanded greatly in the 1960s, both in personnel dedicated to the task of educating handicapped children and in the availability of services to such children, by the early 1970s many children with disabilities were still not receiving special services of any kind. And whereas the special class still was the dominant way of offering special education, the resource room—a classroom that a child could attend for part of the day while being "mainstreamed" for most of the school day—was fast becoming the preferred mode for many children with relatively mild problems in learning.

In 1975, a landmark education law was passed by the U.S. Congress and signed into law by President Gerald Ford—the *Education for All Handicapped Children Act* (often referred to as Public Law 94-142 or EAHCA). Some believe this law to be equally as important in the history of American public education as state laws mandating school attendance or the 1954 United States Supreme Court school desegregation case, *Brown v. Board of Education of Topeka*.[6] The law was enacted in response to advocates for children with disabilities, mainly parents, who were unhappy with the extent and types of special education services being offered in schools nationwide. Many children with disabilities were receiving no services at all, and their parents wanted them to receive special education. Mostly, these unserved children were those with severe or profound disabilities, who had simply been denied access to public schooling. Some children with disabilities were receiving inappropriate services not tailored to their disabilities, or were receiving services without the informed consent of their parents. Some children were served in environments that were more restrictive than necessary—for example, going to special schools far from home when they could attend regular schools in or closer to their neighborhoods, or receiving all of their services in special classes when they could be mainstreamed for at least part of the day.

The 1975 federal law (PL 94-142, or EAHCA) was mandatory. That is, it *required* that if a state wanted to receive *any* federal education monies, then it had to have a plan to offer special education to *all* handicapped children, not just some, and it had to give priority to special education for those with the most severe disabilities. The 1975 law and its accompanying regulations were quite complicated, but the most important provisions were quite straightforward. The basic requirements of federal special education law are summarized in Table 1.1. The primary vehicle for ensuring an appropriate education was the individualized education program (IEP). An IEP was to specify the special education and related services to be provided for each handicapped child.[7]

A common misinterpretation of the law is that it puts the "least restrictive environment" (LRE) first in importance or that it requires the inclusion of all students in regular schools and classrooms. It does neither. It puts a "free, appropriate public education" (FAPE) first and makes LRE a secondary matter. The law was an attempt to ensure, first of all, that all handicapped children would receive an appropriate education at public expense (i.e., free, in the sense of no cost to parents or guardians). A secondary objective was to make sure that the appropriate education would be provided as close to home and in as normal or typical an environment as possible. In determining the LRE for a particular student, the law requires that a full "continuum of alternative placements" (CAP) be considered. The CAP includes the full range of placement options, from residential or hospital placements to special schools, special classes, resource classes, and various options for inclusion in regular classes and neighborhood schools.

When Congress enacted EAHCA in 1975, it knew that special education costs considerably more than general education on a per pupil basis (several times over, on average). The cost was to be paid by a combination of federal, state, and local funds. When the federal law was passed, Congress stated its intention to pick up 40% of the

---

TABLE 1.1   Basic Provisions of Federal Special Education Law

Free, Appropriate Public Education (FAPE): Every student with a disability is entitled to an appropriate education at public expense (at no cost to parents or guardians).

Continuum of Alternative Placements (CAP): Placements ranging from separate special schools, hospital schools, and home instruction to special classes, resource rooms, inclusion in regular classes with supplementary services, and all other placement options must be available to every student with a disability.

Least Restrictive Environment (LRE): Every student with a disability is to be educated in the least restrictive environment that is consistent with his or her educational needs, as close to home as possible, and, insofar as possible, with students without disabilities.

Individualized Education Program (IEP): Every student with a disability is to have a written, individualized education program, which includes a statement of the special services to be provided and the goals of those services.

Note: Many details and provisions of the law are not included in this table, which includes only basic definitions of core requirements of the law.

(*Individuals with Disabilities Education Act,* IDEA)

excess cost, but actual Congressional appropriations never reached a level anywhere near that in the 20th century. The federal share of special education costs became a major issue in the early 21st century.

In the mid-1980s, some seeking to reform special education requirements and practices, including Madeline Will (who was then an Assistant Secretary of Education in the Bureau of Education for the Handicapped) proposed a "Regular Education Initiative" (REI).[8] The REI was an attempt to return responsibility for many or most students with disabilities to regular classroom teachers. The REI of the 1980s became the "full inclusion" movement (FIM) of the 1990s. Full inclusion was the radical proposition that all students, regardless of the nature or severity of their disability, should be placed for most or all of the day in the regular neighborhood schools they would attend if they had no disability.[9]

In 1990 and 1997, the federal special education law was reauthorized by the United States Congress. Its name was changed to the *Individuals with Disabilities Education Act* (IDEA), and some new requirements were added. However, the basic provision of the law remained intact: FAPE, CAP, LRE, and the IEP remained the bedrock of the law, and all other provisions are intended to guarantee these for all students with disabilities.

Contemporary and Perpetual Issues

Some of the controversial issues about special education are both current and perpetual. Universal public education, meaning that all children are required to go to school until they reach a certain age and no student is denied an education, always creates controversial issues. These issues are not easily resolved, and people are bound to differ in their opinions about the best solutions. Barbara Bateman, special educator and legal expert, long ago stated the perpetual issues of "who, how, and where."[10] The questions might be worded as follows:

Who should have the authority to say that a student needs special education? On what basis should they make this judgment?

How should special education differ from general education? What should be its objectives, curricula, and outcomes?

Where should special education be offered? To what extent can it be or should it be a part of the general plan for universal public education?

Of course, there are other who, how, and where questions as well.

Who should teach exceptional children? What personal characteristics should qualify them for the job?

How should teachers be prepared as special educators? Who should train them, and what should they be prepared to do?

Where should special educators practice their craft? With whom must they be prepared to work, and in what contexts should they be expected to function?

Questions in the Puzzle and the Nature of the Dilemma

Whenever a society attempts to provide universal education, special education is an inevitable puzzle to be solved. The puzzle is created by the fact that students differ so markedly in what they have learned and what they can learn by a particular age. The puzzle may be solved in somewhat different ways in different societies, but the questions raised are the same. And the questions always involve trade-offs and risks. That is the nature of any true dilemma—there is no cost-free or risk-free solution.

Special education presents dilemmas because we cannot have things every which way. It is not possible to have the same education for everyone and have special education for some. It is not possible to have different education for those at the extremes of performance, yet have every child educated in a common place or space. So, we are confronted with difficult questions such as the following:

- *Which is a worse mistake in the matter of identifying (or not) an exceptionality:* (a) a *false positive* or (b) a *false negative*? (A false positive means identifying an exceptionality that does not really exist; a false negative means not identifying an exceptionality that does exist.) An absolutely foolproof, error-free system of identification is not possible. The question really is this: Which type of mistake is worse?

- *Which is a worse consequence of a given student's placement:* (a) *removing the student from the mainstream* to meet his or her needs more adequately in a special class or school or (b) *keeping the student in the mainstream* where his or her education will not be the best it can be and where he or she will not receive the intensity of instruction necessary for success? (Removal from the mainstream risks the stigma of separation and missing out on the general education curriculum; placement in the mainstream risks the stigma of being different from others and having a curriculum that is ill-suited to the student's needs.) Remember that both special education and general education can be either poorly practiced or practiced very well. Remember that the answer need not be the same for all students with exceptionalities. Remember further that it is impossible to offer all possible educational curricula and methods in the same place and at the same time. So, the question really is this: Which choice do we think carries the least risk and the greatest probability of benefit for the student?

- *Which is a worse scenario for a student with exceptionalities:* (a) a teacher with little or no special training and little experience teaching a small class or group of students or (b) a teacher with exceptionally good training and a lot of experience teaching a large class or group of students? (Of course, the situation could be reversed, and then the choice would be very easy: a teacher with exceptionally good training and experience and a small class or group would be preferable to a poorly trained and inexperienced teacher with a large class or group.) In the real world we know that teachers may be well trained or poorly trained, experienced or inexperienced, have either small or large classes, be assigned to teach special education or general education. We see the aforementioned contrast or choice between (a) and (b) as one that will sometimes have to be made in deciding what is best for a particular student. The choice really is: What do we know about the teacher and his or her assignment, and which teacher will best serve the student?

■ *Which is a worse mistake in assessing a student's ability to learn a particular task or skill:* (a) *underestimating* what a student can accomplish, and therefore failing to teach a student something he or she could learn or (b) *overestimating* what a student can accomplish, thereby requiring the student to fail repeatedly and squandering time that could have been spent teaching something the student could master? (No foolproof, absolutely accurate, errorless system of assessment has been or can be devised; assessment of a student's capabilities is a matter of experienced human judgment that is less than perfect, and no algorithm yields zero errors.) As in the case of identification of exceptionality, the decision could be a false positive (assuming that the student can learn the task when he or she cannot) or a false negative (assuming that the student cannot learn the task when he or she actually can). The question is really this, for purposes of choosing curriculum or learning goals or expectations: Which kind of error does the least damage to the student?

■ *Which is a worse curriculum for middle-school and secondary-school students with disabilities:* (a) a curriculum that is essentially the same as the one provided non-disabled students or (b) a curriculum that emphasizes skills that the student lacks that he or she will need to function in the community? To deny students with disabilities access to the general education curriculum increases the gap between them and their nondisabled peers in comprehension of core content subjects such as history, English, and science. But focusing on regular academics takes away time needed to train students in life skills, such as time management, money management, job training, and self-advocacy. The question really is this: What information or skills are critical for the long-term well-being of the student with disabilities?

These are certainly not all of the dilemmas involved in special education. We offer them as examples only. Our point is simply that special education very frequently, if not always, involves trade-offs, compromises, and choosing the lesser of two evils. Special education is not by any means unique in this respect. In many areas of our lives—including medical treatment, deciding to end a marriage, or flying in an airplane, for example—we have to weigh one anticipated cost or possible negative outcome against another. In many areas of our lives, there are no guarantees.

Perhaps it is understandable that some people want to simplify the issues or avoid the most difficult questions about special education by assuming that the answer should always be the same, regardless of the student. For example, some may argue that inclusion in general education is always better, regardless of the student involved, or that the same expectations should apply to all students, regardless of their abilities. This solution—always the same answer, regardless of the student— seems egalitarian at first blush. But, to us, it seems to reflect a kind of rigidity, an inflexibility, an unwillingness to come to grips with human exceptionality or a readiness to deny it. The consequence is education that is unfair because it is ill-suited to the individual, especially to the individual who is very discrepant from the norm.

Finally, we note that some cases of exceptionality are so obvious as to make the dilemmas we have sketched entirely avoidable. The most extreme outliers—those with profound disabilities and those who are child prodigies, for example—show differences that rational people cannot deny and that few would argue do not require extraordinary or special education. However, the largest number of students consists of those with less extreme differences, less obvious special needs, those about whom one can argue for either (a) or (b) in any given dilemma. The largest number of students for whom special education is an issue consists of students on the borderline between typical and atypical, and their identification is a matter of fallible judgment. They are the students who present us with the dilemmas we have described; this is an ineradicable challenge that we explain further in the next chapter.

Summary

There are many misconceptions about the puzzle special education presents in our society. Historically, special education has been an attempt to increase the fairness of universal public education for exceptional learners (those with special difficulties or extraordinary abilities in learning). Since 1975, federal law (IDEA, the Individuals with Disabilities Education Act) has required schools to provide special education for all children with disabilities who need it. Special education has its perpetual issues, including these questions: *Who* should be identified for special education? *How* should they be served? *Where* should special education be provided? Providing special education is not an easy puzzle to solve, as it presents difficult dilemmas— difficult choices, none of which is cost-free, risk-free, or the perfect solution.

BOX **1.1**

Case in Point

Here and in each of the following chapters, we offer a composite case in point (constructed from our experience) for you to think about. We have chosen to make our example male and the disability a learning disability simply because male and learning disability are the most common categories involved in special education. However, we hope you will remember that females and other types of disabilities are represented in special education.

Jimmy is now a sixth-grader. He has always gotten along well with his classmates and teachers. He has always seemed to try hard to learn. He does acceptable, grade-level work in every subject except reading. Last year, when he was in the fifth grade, he was reading on the second-grade level. His parents and his teachers were uncertain whether he needed special education. Both his parents and his teachers thought he might just be lagging a little and that if they helped him more and he worked hard enough he'd catch up and be reading on grade level in a year or two. Maybe tutoring in reading is all he needs, his parents thought, but his teachers said he might need special education. His parents and teachers asked, are the hassle, possible stigma, and cost worth the potential benefits of special education? Who will teach him? Where will he go to get this special instruction, and what will he be missing out on in his "regular" classroom in order to get this special education in reading?

REFERENCE NOTES

1. For misconceptions and facts for each category of disability and many special education issues, see Hallahan & Kauffman (2003). For common misconceptions about teaching, see Heward (2003); Kauffman (2002); Sasso (2001). For description of good teaching, see Bateman (2004).

2. National Research Council (2002, p. 57).

3. For more detailed discussion of the history of special education in the United States, see Hendrick & MacMillan (1989); Kauffman (1981); Kauffman & Landrum (in press); MacMillan & Hendrick (1993); Mann (1979); Sarason & Doris (1979).

4. Singer (1988, p. 416).

5. The change of name to ARC is indicative of the negative light cast on labels and any reference to special education. We find such attempts at political correctness ironic and sad because they work to defeat the very purpose for which they are intended—to cast people who are mentally retarded in a positive light rather than to view their condition as something shameful that must be sugarcoated or hidden.

6. See Sarason & Doris (1979).

7. See Bateman & Linden (1998); Huefner (2000); and Yell (1998) for detailed discussion of the law in its 1997 version. For updates on legal issues in special education, see the Website maintained by legal expert Dixie Snow Huefner and click on "Chapter Updates": http://www.ed.utah.edu/~huefner/sped-law/spdlawbk.htm or www.wrightslaw.com.

8. See Stainback & Stainback (1984, 1991) and Will (1986) for early statements on the Regular Education Initiative.

9. See Fuchs & Fuchs (1994); Hall (2002); Kauffman & Hallahan (1995, 1997, 2005); Kavale & Forness (2000a); and Mock & Kauffman (2005) for description and discussion of the full inclusion movement. See Heward (2003) for discussion of faulty notions about teaching and learning that are popular in education and undermine special education's effectiveness.

10. Bateman (1994).

2 Measurement of Educational Performance

Who needs special education? It all depends on how one "measures up" against an expectation. It is only by measurement and comparison to a group or another standard or expectation that someone can be seen as needing something different from the typical. The concept of measurement is fundamental to the idea of special education—only by measuring what students can do or have achieved can we recognize their need for something atypical. Measurement is basic to any contemporary society, and it is important to think about how measurement of educational performance is related to measurement of other things.

We begin this chapter by explaining why measurement in education is particularly problematic, including *what* should be measured, *how* it should be measured, and how *accurate* the measurement is. We then discuss statistical distributions, including the issues of why distributions are important, where an obtained measurement falls in a distribution, and the meaning of an obtained measurement. Finally, we consider how special education can and should change the educational performance of individual exceptional learners, both those with disabilities and those who are gifted.

A lot of the misunderstanding of exceptional learners and special education comes from misunderstanding measurement in education. Perhaps it is easier for most people to understand the measurement of physical attributes or performance in sports than it is to understand measurement of academic achievement or intelligence. However, because many of the same principles apply to the measurement of anything, we sometimes rely on examples of the measurement of things other than educational performance.

The Problem of Measurement in Education

Measurement is readily accepted in many areas of our lives, but it is particularly problematic in education. However, regardless of the area or performance to be measured, whether it is education, construction, sports, or science, the following questions apply:

- What is to be measured?
- How will it be measured?

- How accurate is the measurement?
- What is a statistical distribution?
- Where does the obtained measurement fall in a distribution?
- What is the meaning of the measurement?

Special education presents one additional question:

- What should be the effect of special education on the individual exceptional learner?

The answers to these questions are not always obvious, at least not when the measurement involves education. In fact, different ways of answering these questions have often sparked controversy and conflict among educators and politicians. The subtleties of educational measurement are many. Some entire textbooks, graduate courses of study, professional conferences, and technical journals are devoted wholly to the topic. Some educators have dedicated their entire professional careers to the study of measurement. Nevertheless, we will attempt to distill a very broad and complex topic into a few pages of explanation.

Our purpose here is to provide a description in plain language of the most fundamental ideas about measuring educational performance.[1]

What Is to Be Measured?

Both educators and the public at large have many different ideas about just what is important to measure in education. What information, facts, or abilities should students be expected to have at a particular age or grade level? Should all students of a particular age or grade level be expected to know or do the same things? That is, should there be a standard set of expectations or requirements? If so, what should they be, and who should set or select them? Should exceptional learners be held to the same standards as other students? Measurement in special education can only be understood in the context of measurement in general education.

These are often questions about which emotions run high and arguments are heated. Measurement has a lot to do with holding schools and teachers accountable for students' learning. Accountability is a very controversial issue—especially for exceptional learners. Some educators have proposed a core curriculum—information that is assumed to be important for all children to learn in school.[2] But, what should be included in the core? Regardless of what anyone suggests, someone in the school district—a parent, teacher, superintendent—is virtually certain to disagree. What someone considers important, central, or indispensable knowledge is probably related to his or her own education and culture.

Much of the controversy about what should be taught—and, therefore, what should be measured—involves information about history. Whose history? Taught from whose perspective? Likewise, literature is often controversial. Whose books should be read? What should be taught about these literary works?[3] In science, questions inevitably arise about what students should be taught and expected to know about scientific methods and principles. Evolution versus creationism, for example, is often a matter debated by school boards, teachers, parents, and students. And if these are controversial issues for typical students, they are even more controversial for exceptional learners, most of whom have learning problems.

We are tempted to see the controversies about what to measure as applying only to the upper grades and only to certain topics, to more advanced study of history, science, and literature, for example. However, controversy is also common regarding more basic skills in reading, writing, and calculating. What reading skills are important: Letter-sound correspondence or whole-word recognition? Oral or silent reading? Decoding or comprehension? When it comes to writing, what spelling and grammatical constructions should be expected or demanded? In mathematical calculating, what operations (e.g., addition, subtraction, multiplication, division) should be taught? What level of precision should be required? Should calculators be allowed? What applications of mathematical principles should be expected? Which is assumed to be more important, the process of obtaining an answer or the answer itself? And what level of precision should be expected (i.e., what responses or range of answers will be judged "correct")?

Then there is the matter of social skills and other behavioral characteristics related to school success. How skillful is the student in relating to peers and authority figures? How long is the student able to sustain attention to school work and other things? How assertive, aggressive, morose, depressed, domineering, self-assured, and/or accepting of others is the student, for example? How do we assess emotional intelligence and behavioral acceptability? What standards of conduct should be expected or imposed? Should all students, including exceptional learners, be disciplined in the same manner?

You can no doubt expand the list of controversies about what should be taught and measured. And you probably see that the controversies are made more complex and nearly intractable when we consider (a) the age or grade at which we should measure any of these skills or knowledge and (b) the range of learners at any given age or grade who should participate in the measures. Some people think that we should not "hurry" children, that we should not have the expectation that nearly all children will read by the age of 6 years, for example. Others believe that if a child is not reading by the age of 6 years then we should be very concerned and take special steps to help the child learn to read. Some educators and policy makers use the word *all* (as in "all children should know letter-sound correspondence by the age of ___") but clearly do not consider children with severe disabilities to be a part of that *all*. Others consider the full range of children and want *all* to be used to mean each and every child, regardless of his or her level of ability or disability.

We note also that in some cases people argue that something other than the student's performance is the most important outcome. For example, some people may suggest that the *process* of education, not what students can demonstrate they have learned, is most important. They may feel that engaging students in hands-on experiences, self-directed projects, and so on is critically important. We agree that it is important to consider the emotional climate of the classroom and the extent to which students are engaged in interesting and self-directed activities, but these factors alone are not sufficient. Students must also be able to demonstrate what they have learned.

Others may argue that parental satisfaction or involvement is at least as important as, if not more important than, the child's performance. They may feel that schools must convince parents that what is happening at school is important for their children. We agree that parents should be satisfied with their children's schools, but we doubt that parental satisfaction is well founded if students are not learning much at school.

And still others may question why more time is not spent on children's moral or character development. They may argue that the current emphasis on academic standards leaves little room in the curriculum for focusing on students' development of morals, ethics, and values. They believe that students must be taught right from wrong or be given precepts for deciding moral issues. We agree that students should be taught moral and ethical values, but we do not consider learning such values to be incompatible with learning other content. In fact, we believe that moral and ethical values have adequate meaning only in the context of academic competence.[4]

Understandably, people are often confused about standards—how they are set and who is to meet them. Exceptional learners who need special education raise particular concerns about standards. Many children with disabilities will be able to meet "universal" standards, but some obviously will not. For many gifted children, the typical standards are ridiculously easy to meet, too low to offer any real challenge.

Deciding *what* to measure is a matter requiring careful judgment. It is not an easy judgment, and there is always the danger of being wrong—choosing to measure knowledge and skills that are somehow inappropriate or trivial for the particular child.

Special education is an attempt to ensure that good judgment is used in the selection of *what* to measure. It represents the desire to make sure that the content of education and the basis of accountability are appropriate for the child's characteristics. It is the realization that all students cannot be and should not be expected to learn the same things, but that realistic challenges are important. It is the understanding that the student's performance, not something else, is the most important thing to measure.

What Tool(s) Will Be Used for Measuring?

In some lines of work or activity, it is easy to see how we should measure performance. Few people have difficulty understanding the best way to measure how far or how high someone can jump, how fast they can run a certain distance, or how much weight they can lift. And many human characteristics, such as height, weight, or age, can be measured in a very straightforward way. True, one has to consider the specifics of what is being measured (e.g., standing long jump or running long jump; high jump or pole vault) and the particular scale (e.g., meters or feet, kilograms or pounds). But there is virtually no complaint about the scale of measurement or the particular tools used to measure.

However, measuring educational achievement and estimating educational potential are anything but straightforward. Some people think a standardized test is the tool that should be used, whereas others consider standardized tests to be bad instruments. Every way of measuring has certain advantages and disadvantages. Useful measurement is necessary for judging whether special education is working—whether it is effectively helping the student, especially in comparison to his or her past performance. Comparisons to norms are important for knowing how well many students are doing compared to others and to "universal" standards. It is important to know how a student is doing in class; how he or she is progressing in instructional materials; and how she or he is getting along in a job, higher education, and community life. The important considerations for special education are that the multiple tools used for measurement are right for the questions being posed and for the student whose progress is being assessed.

How Accurate Is the Measurement?

Every measurement contains a margin of error. This is a way of saying that no measurement is *absolutely* accurate. Every measurement is an estimate of a hypothetical "true" measure. Nevertheless, our measurement of some things can be extremely precise—so precise that the error of measurement is infinitesimal. These extremely precise measurements are characteristics of tool-making and many of the physical sciences. For other things, our measurement is often more clearly just a "ball park" estimate. In education and psychology, for example, measurement is much less precise than is usually the case in sports or physics.

Measurements that do not represent absolute precision can, nevertheless, be extremely helpful. Consider some examples from everyday life. A sign saying that a given city is 5 miles down the road is very helpful, although the town might actually be a little more or less than 5 miles away. A radio announcer might say that it is 80 degrees Fahrenheit (F) outside the studio. We understand that it might actually be 80.5 or 79.7, but that doesn't keep us from getting a pretty good idea how warm it is. An announcement of 80 degrees F means that most people would consider it a warm day and dress accordingly. The fact that measurement contains some uncertainty, whether in transportation schedules, time, or temperature, doesn't keep us from relying on the estimate for making decisions.

But, of course, the important question is how much uncertainty, how much imprecision, how much "slop" in a measure is acceptable before the measure becomes useless. That all depends on the nature and purpose of the measurement. For precision tools and certain professional or Olympic sporting performances, for example, the measurement may need to be extremely precise. For other measurements, such as distances between cities reported on maps and road signs, "intelligence" or psychological well-being, for example, we typically are willing to live with a much lower level of precision, and for good reasons. First, the tools for measuring some things with great precision haven't been developed. Examples are tests of intelligence and achievement. Second, sometimes an extreme level of precision in measurement isn't worth reporting. Extreme precision can actually be distracting because it is more information than we need. Examples would be distances on maps and road signs given to several decimal places. Third, we sometimes find a relatively low level of precision helpful, even though we know there is substantial error in it. Examples are time, temperature, and intelligence.

Some measures of psychological characteristics or educational achievement are frequently misunderstood. The late scientist Stephen Jay Gould described the misunderstanding of measures of intelligence in one of his books, *The Mismeasure of Man.* Gould was not against measuring intelligence, nor did he assume that intelligence can be measured only in meaningless or unhelpful ways. He just objected to the idea that intelligence is a fixed, innate characteristic. He also objected to the notion that someone's tested IQ is extremely accurate. The fact is that achievement tests and IQ (which, it can be argued, is just a type of achievement test) are neither extremely accurate nor unchangeable. Even so, they are helpful in estimating what a person knows and can be expected to do or to learn in the short term.

In the social sciences, tests have a *standard error,* which is an estimate of the range within which a student's true score falls. That is, the standard error of a test tells us that the obtained score (let's say an IQ of 100) is *probably* accurate or true within a given range (let's say, + or – 5 points). For example, someone's true score might actually be 100, but there's a very high chance that their true score falls somewhere between 95 and 105 (if the standard error of the test is 5). The estimated error, + or – a certain number, is commonly given in reporting results of a poll (e.g., an exit poll may be reported as showing that the vote for a certain candidate is 48%, + or – 3 percentage points). The way the standard error is calculated isn't really important here. The point is simply that for certain tests, we can calculate an estimate of the accuracy of the test. For some devices, such as behavioral observations and interviews, it is impossible to calculate an accuracy estimate in the usual way. We must rely on a more subjective estimate of accuracy.

Educators are expected to make educated guesses about students. "Educated" guess means a guess based on the best available data. This is why we have testing and other forms of assessment—to help us make better-informed judgments or guesses. Special educators are expected to make judgments about students who are not typical in some way, who have special needs that most children do not, and/or who are at the fringes of performances or characteristics that are relevant to schooling. No instrument used by special educators is absolutely accurate. Judgments can be wrong, too, even informed ones. But the reality is that refusing to make a judgment merely ensures that special needs will not be met. For special education purposes, the more accurate the measure the better, because the decisions made about a student on the basis of measurement are extremely important. We do not want, nor do we feel it is defensible, to identify a student for special education or deny special education to a student on the basis of measurement that is very inaccurate. That is why we should always use multiple measures in making special education decisions.

What Is a Statistical Distribution?

Every kind of measurement results in a statistical distribution. And statistical distributions are the basis for deciding in most cases what is "normal." We consider 98.6 degrees F (or, we could say about 99 degrees F) to be normal body temperature simply because that's the temperature obtained for *most* people who aren't sick. We judge the birth weight of babies to be normal because of what *most* babies weigh at birth. We judge birth weight to be low when it is below the *average* for human babies. Height, weight, eyesight, hearing, age at death, intelligence, and all other human characteristics are judged normal (expected, typical, average) or abnormal by comparing an individual to a large number of other people—to a statistical distribution. The same is true for special education. Normal or typical learners are those whose scores on whatever we believe is a good measure are about average. Exceptional learners, or those who need special education, are statistical outliers—their scores are at the extreme of the distribution, not close to average.

All statistical distributions have some shared mathematical properties. The *range* of a distribution is the numerical distance from lowest to highest score. The range can be small or large, but there always is a range, or you don't have a statistical distribution. The *mode* is the most frequent score, the one obtained most often. The *median* is the middle score or midpoint in a distribution. Half the scores are always above and half below the median. The *mean* is the arithmetic average of the scores, obtained by adding all the scores together and dividing by the number of scores. The median, mean, and mode are sometimes referred to together as measures of *central tendency*—indicators of the typical or average individual or group in a distribution. If we draw a curve based on a typical or normal statistical distribution, the curve is symmetrical, like the one shown in Figure 2.1. The figure could represent a curve or distribution for any performance in which we are interested (e.g., the reading performance of 10-year-olds attending public schools). Measuring a lot of individuals' ability on just about anything produces a distribution that looks somewhat like the one depicted in Figure 2.1—symmetrical, with a single highest point.

Consider Figure 2.1 as an example. First, notice that the scores range from 1 to 15. Suppose that you and 112 other people were given a 15-point test, and the scores on it were distributed as shown in Figure 2.1. What the figure shows is that only one person got a score of 1, and only one person got a score of 15 (that's 2 people accounted for). Two people got a score of 14, and two got a score of 2 (total = 6 people). Three got a score of 3 and three a score of 13 (total = 12). Six people scored 4 and six scored 12 (total = 24). Nine people got a score of 5, and nine got 11 (total =

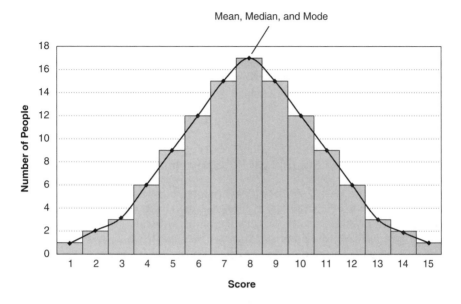

FIGURE 2.1   **Mean, Median, and Mode**

42). Twelve people earned a score of 6, and twelve scored 10 (total = 66). Fifteen people got 7 correct and fifteen got 9 correct (total = 96). Finally, seventeen people earned a score of 8 (total = 113). In Figure 2.1, the mean (arithmetic average), the median (middle score), and the mode (most frequent score) are all the same score— 8. In a *normal* statistical distribution (the kind of distribution most often obtained when a human characteristic is measured in a large number of people) the median, mean, and mode are always the same score. Also, as you can see, the curve is just a way of representing and smoothing out a bar graph showing how many individuals got each score.

A statistical distribution shows all the scores, from the lowest to the highest, and the number of individuals getting each score. In a normal distribution, only a very small number of individuals get the highest scores, and only a very few get the lowest. The vast majority of individuals get a score somewhere between the top and the bottom scores, with the largest number getting a score about midway between the highest and the lowest. Of course, not all distributions are normal-looking. For example, some have a couple of scores tied for the most frequent (these are called multi-modal), and some are lopsided (these are called skewed). Even for non-normal distributions, however, there is always a mean (arithmetical average) and a median (a midpoint). There is always a top 25 percent (or choose any percent you like; the same applies) and a bottom 10 percent (again, choose whatever percent you wish, as it works) of the individuals measured, regardless of how high or low the mean and median are on the device used for measurement. But here we are only considering normal-looking or nearly normal distributions because they are the most typical kind related to special education.

Special education is designed for students who are at the extremes of a distribution, whose scores are either exceptionally low or extremely high. The scores of students for whom special education is designed are not near the average, whether we are concerned about academic achievement in a given subject, social behavior, learning speed, language ability, physical abilities, vision, hearing, or any combination of these abilities.

Why Be Concerned About Statistical Distributions?

So, why should we discuss statistical distributions? Simply put, statistical distributions of achievement or performance are the basis for special education; to understand special education, one must understand statistical distributions. Special education is designed for and is necessary for individuals whose scores on tests or whose performances on other types of measures are at the extremes—much lower or higher than is typical.

Consider Figure 2.1 further. Imagine that it represents a very large number of individuals, so that the numbers on the vertical axis represent hundreds or thousands of people. We *could* assume that a score of two or less (on this scale of scores from 1–15) should be the criterion for identifying students as being in need of special education because of a disability. However, we *could* just as well choose a score of 3 or less or 4 or less as indicating disability. The criterion we choose would make a big difference in how many students qualify. Then consider the other end of the distribution, the right-hand side. What should be the criterion for giftedness? A score of 15, 14, 13, or 12? Are these the scores that *should* indicate the need for special education? We have just used examples based on the hypothetical distribution of test scores shown in Figure 2.1, but the same basic idea applies regardless of the test or measurement. Read on, and you will see that the criteria selected for indicating a need for special education are somewhat arbitrary and can be changed, regardless of who chooses them.

Where a score falls in a statistical distribution is a critically important matter in deciding whether special education is appropriate or a mistake. We caution here that some measures may not be associated with known statistical distributions (e.g., portfolios of students' work). These measures are of value only if we make an *implicit* judgment of a distribution. Without an implicit or explicit distribution that we use for comparing an individual's score to the scores to others, a score or judgment is meaningless.

A final point to remember about distributions in education is that the things we measure are almost all characterized by a *continuous distribution.* In a continuous distribution, the thing that is measured can vary from a little to a lot, with very fine gradations possible. Height, weight, and age, for example, are continuously distributed; someone can be very short or tall, and it is possible to measure height very precisely. Furthermore, someone can be considered about average in height, sort of short, or on the tallish side.

However, some things can be classified into categories with only two choices: yes or no. For example, we could say that something does (yes) or does not (no) exist or that someone has (yes) or has not (no) met a particular standard. We could score something as 1 or 0 to indicate, for example, that something is (1) or isn't (0) present, and so on. We call such things *discrete* categories. One example is citizenship; you either are or are not a citizen of a particular country. Another is gender; you are either male or female. (We do recognize that very occasionally gender is mixed, but that does not keep us from recognizing that in the vast majority of cases one is either male or female, not somewhat one or the other.) Another example is pregnancy; a woman either is or is not pregnant, and hence we see it as funny to consider someone "sort of pregnant" or "a little bit pregnant." Of course, we realize that children and adults joking around may say a woman is "a little bit" pregnant, meaning that the pregnancy is just beginning to show, but at the same time we understand that pregnancy is a yes/no or is/isn't discrete category.

We may, for sure, categorize people or things by establishing cut points on a continuous distribution. That is, we can, and sometimes do, establish discrete categories based on scores on a continuous distribution. This is usually the way people come up with criterion-referenced tests or standards in education. But in other areas of our lives, too, we often establish categories. For example, we might have categories of tall/short, obese/not obese, gifted/average, or old-enough-to-vote/not-old-enough-to-vote—even though height, the ratio of height to weight, intelligence or other ability, and age are continuous distributions. This is an important concept for special education. We return later to the notion of categories of disability based on continuous distributions.

We realize that sometimes it is important to measure how an individual student's performance changes over time without making any comparison to how other students perform. We simply compare individuals to themselves. However, in all cases comparisons to others are also eventually important. That is, we always want to know how what a student can do compares to typical expectations. The only way to do this is to consider the statistical distribution that we inevitably get from measuring a large number of individuals. True, every student needs to be seen as an individual, and self-comparisons have a critical role to play in evaluating progress, but no student is an island—a person with no connection to others. Group comparisons are ultimately needed to make self-comparisons meaningful.

By giving so much attention to measurement we risk the criticism that we are overly concerned about numbers and test scores. We do *not* mean to imply that the essence of a child's identity can be captured in a single score, or even a set of scores. We do mean to acknowledge, though, that measures, whether they be test scores or observations, are critical to special education because by definition an exceptional learner is one who differs from the norm—the average, the typical.

Where Does the Obtained Measurement Fall in Its Distribution?

The score for an individual (or a group of individuals) is always compared, implicitly or explicitly, to a statistical distribution. Without such comparison, we simply have no way of judging whether an individual or group is achieving about what we should expect (i.e., about average, as indicated by known or assumed central tendency and standard deviation), way low, or way high.

Reasonable expectations are always set by comparison to what most people in a group can do or the way most people in a group behave. The group may be defined by age, sex, experience, prior performance, or some combination of these (e.g., American boys ages 7–10 who have been playing organized soccer for at least a year). The group may be defined very broadly (loosely) or very narrowly (i.e., very tightly or specifically by a combination of many criteria). Our point is simply that without comparison to a reference group with a known or assumed distribution we have no basis for judgment of the meaning or significance of a performance. Distributions help us know whether a child is ok and "on track" or whether we should be concerned because something seems to be wrong. This is true whether the distribution is of growth, height:weight ratio, blood fats, white blood cell count, or some aspect of educational performance or social skill.

A given measure might be set up to reflect pass-fail. In this case, a criterion value is set, and students are expected to reach it. The particular measurement or the student's score doesn't matter much, except that it either does or does not meet the criterion or standard. People are tempted to believe that a distribution isn't really important in this case. However, the criterion or standard isn't just picked at random. The people who set the criterion or standard have to consider what most individuals can do, and therefore what is reasonable to expect. The standard could be set so high that nearly everyone fails or so low that nearly everyone passes. Choosing the standard or criterion is a matter of judging what percent of a group must fail before the criterion is said to be set too high or what percent must pass before the criterion is said to be too low. Our point stands: The distribution is always, inevitably, and rightly, the basis for judgment.

We return to another point we made earlier: We often and for good reason develop categories based on continuous distributions. Remember that we could set up a dichotomy of tall/not tall, even though height is a continuous distribution. And sometimes it may be useful to do that (e.g., to have a "tall man's shop," a height or weight criterion for riding a pony or getting on an amusement park ride, or an age criterion for buying alcoholic beverages or voting in an election for public office). But there are some inevitable results of dichotomizing or categorizing on the basis of a continuous distribution. First, there are always some "borderline" cases, individuals who are "sort-of-but-not-quite," who just miss the criterion for classification. And our measurement, regardless of how accurate we try to make it, has a margin of error, so there is always some ambiguity for cases that are on or very near the border. There is simply no way to avoid this problem; it goes with the measurement of any continuous variable. We can, like the legal system in the case of buying alcohol or voting, choose to ignore this ambiguity—just pick an objective criterion like age and stick with it regardless of other considerations. But in most cases related to special education, which deal with learning and behavior, we think it is more responsible to use some clinical judgment in borderline cases as well as numerical information from tests.

Second—and this point is particularly important for thinking about special education—the closer we set the criterion to the central tendency (either above or below the mean, median, or mode) the larger the number and percentage of cases that will be "borderline." The reason this is true is that as you move toward the central part of a distribution more cases (individuals) are involved, meaning also that more are on the verge or borderline of the criterion.

The phenomenon we have just described—more cases of uncertainty, more borderline cases as you move toward the central part of a distribution—is one of the reasons people are reluctant to practice prevention. Prevention requires catching cases early, before they are far from the central tendency in reading, social behavior, and so on. But catching cases early means, inevitably, moving the criterion for doing something about it closer to the central tendency, and, therefore, (a) serving a larger number of individuals, (b) encountering more borderline cases, and (c) dealing with more uncertainty about these cases. These realities cannot be avoided.

Special education requires deciding where in a distribution of achievement or performance we think the criterion should be set for special intervention. If exceptional children are to receive education or other services different from what is received by others, then we have to choose a line or place in the distribution for delivery of that service. Failure to draw a line simply means that nothing special, extra, or different will be done for the student; it precludes special education. Someone can argue that the line or criterion should be higher or lower and still recognize that a line is necessary. However, when someone argues that we should not draw a line at all, then they are arguing for the abandonment of special education, because it is impossible to have something special or different without having a line—unless individuals are picked at random for special treatment, which makes no sense at all. True, any point we pick on a distribution can be criticized as arbitrary or wrong. Establishing a criterion means taking the risk of choosing a bad one. But not establishing a criterion means being wrong for certain.

What Is the Meaning of an Obtained Measurement?

People often misinterpret measurements, regardless of the nature of the measure. They may misunderstand the meaning of a term having to do with any measurement: mean, median, mode, range, percentile, and so on. However, misunderstanding of the meaning of an obtained measurement may be even more common than misunderstanding of measurement itself. By "obtained" measurement related to education, we mean the number attached to the test. People often misinterpret a particular test score as absolutely accurate or as reflecting something inherent and unchangeable

(Stephen Jay Gould's point in *The Mismeasure of Man*). They may also overgeneralize (e.g., conclude that failing one test or criterion means failing at everything important). They may dismiss a test, observation, or other measurement as trivial or unimportant when it is not.

The critical issue in educational measurement is, of course, what you make of it—the score or other obtained measure. How do we know what it means? There are no set rules for determining what an obtained measurement means, but all of the questions we have addressed to this point in the chapter must be taken into consideration. There is no substitute for thinking about what was measured—why and how the obtained measurement compares to others' performance.

Special education demands that educators, psychologists, and parents together try to figure out what the measurements of a child's performance mean. The job is difficult and subject to error, so care is required. The task is to try to figure out what the obtained measurements mean with respect to (a) the importance of the information, (b) the child's comparison to others, (c) the child's trajectory or direction, and (d) the likelihood that the child needs special accommodations or specialized teaching in particular areas because he or she is way above or below expectations for typical learners.

How Can and Should Special Education Change Performance?

Most people would like to see average educational performance improve, whether the average is represented by the mean or the median. This is possible, and it is probable, too, if most students are taught better.[5] But many people also want to decrease the discrepancies between high and low scorers—that is, to shrink the variance (dispersion), to make the population more homogeneous (individuals more like each other in achievement). The only way to do this, however, is to totally neglect, if not deliberately inhibit, the learning of the fastest students while pulling out all the stops to help low achievers. An alternative is to simply not include the low performers in the distribution.

To understand why a distribution will become more spread out if we simply speed up all learners, it is necessary only to understand the concept of rate of progress. You could imagine cars, horses, planes, or trains moving at different speeds (rates), or you could just think about the fact that different students learn any given thing at different speeds. For any given skill or topic, some learners are faster than others. Some are a *lot* faster than the average, and some are a *lot* slower. Most students are approximately average. For whatever reason, the fastest learners pick up the information or skill in a very short period of time and with very few trials; the slowest learners take a long time and many trials to learn the same thing, if they are able to learn it at all. (A few children can never reasonably be expected to read.) The *rate* of acquisition of knowledge or skill involving any performance approximates a normal distribution.

If you start with a normal distribution and allow the students (or cars, horses, planes, or trains) to proceed at different rates, then they spread out with time. The longer they go at that rate, the more spread out they get. It is not difficult to understand why some people won't like the first results of speeding up everyone, because if we do this we will increase the discrepancies between high and low achievers—we've then done just the *opposite* of homogenizing student performance.

So, how *should* special education change a distribution? And what *should* special education do for an individual student's score? It should simply keep low achievers from scoring as low as they would otherwise and help high scorers score higher than they would otherwise. It is important to recognize that actual discrepancies between the slowest learners and the average may stay the same or even increase if all learners are given equitable treatment, but without special education for students with disabilities the discrepancies would be even greater. It is also important to recognize that no education—neither good special education nor good general education, nor any education that can be provided—will eliminate all failure or eliminate the lower part of the distribution.

We should also be wary of the comparisons people make in evaluating special education. Sometimes people suggest that special education should be judged successful to the extent that the mean or distribution for exceptional learners approximates that of learners who are not exceptional. This is clearly an unreasonable comparison because exceptional learners are by definition extremely different from the typical student and can never reasonably be expected as a group to perform like those without exceptionalities.[6]

The only comparison that makes sense in evaluating special education is the difference between what exceptional learners achieve *with* compared to *without* special education. Often, this comparison is impossible because we are not allowed (and for good reason) to deny special education to a student who we think needs it. We are ethically prohibited from doing a true experiment to see whether or to what extent special education "works." So we are often left having to make comparisons to neglected groups (those who needed special education but for some reason did not receive it) that were not randomly assigned or to suppose what would have happened to individuals had they not received special education (based on our knowledge of what happened in the past when special education was not provided). Or, it is possible to use sophisticated statistical designs to try to find out whether special education improves performance.[7] Special education appears to do just that—improve performance over what it would have been without special education.

We remind readers that special education involves not only learners with disabilities but also those whose abilities are extraordinarily high. Giving equitable attention to exceptionally fast learners means providing them with extra teaching and, in many cases, an accelerated curriculum.

Special education *should* result in the failure of fewer children by standards that are reasonable for them. It also *should* improve the performance of individual students over what it would have been otherwise, had they not received special education.

Summary

Measurement in education presents many problems, including what is to be measured, how it will be measured, and the accuracy of measurement. It is important to understand statistical distributions, where a measurement falls in a distribution, and what the obtained measurement means. Special education also requires that we think about how we *can* and how we *should* try to change a distribution and what the effect of special education on the individual exceptional learner should be. Although exceptional learners may be compared to themselves, ultimately it is important also to consider how they compare to others. Comparing the achievement of students with disabilities to those without disabilities is unfair and irrational. However, special education should result in students doing better than they would have done without it.

BOX **2.1**

Case in Point

Jimmy's parents agreed to allow testing to see whether he qualified for special education, so a school psychologist did some testing. She gave Jimmy a standardized, individual intelligence test and a standardized reading test. She found that Jimmy's IQ is 114, a high average score that suggests he should be reading on grade level. She found that Jimmy's reading level was second grade and that 93 percent of fifth graders did better than he on this reading test. So, it looked to the psychologist, Jimmy's teachers, and his parents that he qualified for special education and that it would be helpful. No one knows precisely *why* Jimmy has this problem in reading, but his failure to read adequately for his age and IQ are not in question.

REFERENCE NOTES

1. For more in-depth and technical discussion of measurement and statistical distributions see Gould (1996a, 1996b); for more in-depth discussion of educational measurement see Popham (2000, 2002).
2. For example, Hirsch (1987).
3. Ravitch (2003).
4. See Huitt & Vessel (2003) for discussion of character development; see Hirsch (1996) and Kohn (1999) for broader discussion of educational process, parental satisfaction, and moral education.
5. See Engelmann (1997).

6. For example, the President's Commission on Excellence in Special Education (2002) stated, "Sadly, few children placed in special education close the achievement gap to a point where they can read and learn like their peers" (p. 3) and "The ultimate test of the value of special education is that, once identified, children close the achievement gap with their peers" (p. 4). These statements are obviously at odds with reality, as noted by Kauffman (in press a, in press b).

7. For example, a statistical study showed that students achieved more with than without special education (Hanushek, Kain, & Rivkin, 2002).

3 The Nature of Educational Disabilities

What is it about exceptional learners (or exceptional children) that sets them apart from others? As we saw in Chapter 2, a quantitative difference, which may be perceived also as a qualitative difference, sets the exceptional child apart from those who are typical. As we stated in *Exceptional Learners,* our introductory text in special education,

> The study of exceptional learners is the study of *differences.* The exceptional learner is different in some way from the average. In very simple terms, such a person may have problems or special talents in thinking, seeing, hearing, speaking, socializing, or moving. More often than not, he or she has a combination of special abilities or disabilities.[1]

True, we go on to say in our text, special education is also the study of *similarities* or *commonalities* among learners. It's important to understand that exceptional learners don't differ from the typical in *every* way. They are, in fact, typical in some respects. Although a child or youth may have disabilities in some specific areas, his or her abilities are at least as important to recognize. And just because a learner is gifted in one area of performance doesn't mean that he or she is gifted in every way.

Nevertheless, the differences that characterize exceptional learners cannot be denied. Suggesting that children are "more alike than different" does not hide their differences or mean that these differences can be ignored. These differences are the foundation for definition; they must be recognized and addressed if the exceptional learner is to be treated fairly. However, educators are called upon to use their judgment about the meaning of various measurements (quantitative data) and disability. Barbara Bateman and Mary Anne Linden stated this as the first "commandment" of the *Individuals with Disabilities Education Act* (IDEA), the primary federal law involving special education:

> I. Thou shalt base all eligibility decisions on professional judgment, not on quantitative formulae.[2]

Disability, then, is not *simply* a matter of scoring at a certain level on a test or tests. The test information or quantitative formula may *inform* judgment. In fact, subjective or "clinical" judgment without more objective and quantitative scores is likely to be very unreliable. But in the end disability for special education purposes is a professional judgment, based on accumulated evidence that a student needs to learn something other than the general education curriculum *or* needs instruction other than that which can be provided by the regular classroom teacher *or both.* Failure to make the judgment—to draw a line, to take action that recognizes the difference— merely denies the child special services.

Children can be different in many ways that are important for their education. Just because a child has a disability or a special talent does not *necessarily* mean that he or she needs special education. The difference must matter for *educational* purposes if special education is to be required. Many or most of the differences shown by exceptional children *are* relevant to education. If these differences are not recognized and accommodated, the children's education suffers.

Moreover, all people—children and adults—need affiliation for at least some of the time with others who share important characteristics or preferences with them. This is why we have clubs, fraternities, sororities, and various organizations catering to age groups, ethnic groups, veteran status, females or males, and so on. Failure to recognize the need of students to be, at least some of the time, with other students with disabilities like theirs closes the door to the development of a supportive disability culture.[3] We are *not* suggesting that students with disabilities should always be taught in separate programs or schools with others who have disabilities. We *are* suggesting that there is potential benefit in congregating students with like disabilities for some purposes and that those responsible for educating students must consider the full continuum of alternative placements (CAP) for students with disabilities. The full continuum is mandated by law. It ranges from separate special schools to inclusion in regular classes in the neighborhood school with supplementary services as needed.

In the following sections, we describe some of the major categories of exceptionality in which special education is typically involved. We note that although categories may be created or abolished in federal or state statutes, all of the exceptionalities we discuss are categories that teachers, psychologists, and others who work with children in schools recognize as important. Exceptionality for special education purposes may involve any one or any combination of the difficulties or exceptional abilities we list. An exceptional child may have special difficulty in:

- Thinking (cognition)
- Learning an academic subject or subjects (achievement not consistent with cognitive ability)
- Focusing and sustaining attention or being reasonably still and accessible to teaching
- Recognizing and controlling emotions or behavior
- Communicating through speech
- Hearing
- Seeing

■ Moving or maintaining physical well-being
■ Severe disabilities or multiple areas of disability (i.e., extreme disabilities or several disabilities in combination)

Children may be exceptional because they have special gifts or talents, usually in thinking, academics, arts, or sports. These gifts or talents may occur in combination (e.g., a child may be gifted intellectually, academically, and in sports) and may occur along with a disability (e.g., a child may be gifted intellectually, yet have a learning disability in a particular academic area or be intellectually gifted but have a physical disability).

We note here that multiple disabilities may involve specific brain disorders or dysfunction. These are relatively rare disorders and include such specific syndromes (clusters of specific characteristics) as autism (or autistic spectrum disorders), traumatic brain injury, and other syndromes that typically entail multiple problems.

We next offer brief definitions of exceptionalities that often require special education. A full discussion of the definition of each exceptionality is beyond the scope of this book, as is detailed discussion of causes and remediation. Our purpose here is to describe common exceptionalities and comment briefly on why special education may be required as a response. For more detailed discussion of each exceptionality, we recommend consulting an introductory text in special education, such as our *Exceptional Learners: Introduction to Special Education.*[4]

Three Important Points About Disabilities and Exceptionalities

Distinction Between *Dis*ability and *In*ability

A critical point about *dis*ability is its distinction from *in*ability. Every disability is an inability, but not every inability is a disability. In other words, disability is a subset of inability. *A disability is an inability to do something that most people, with typical maturation, opportunity, or instruction, can do.* For example, most 6-month-olds cannot walk or talk. They have an inability that is age appropriate, but if that inability persists well past the time that most children learn to walk and talk, then we consider the inability a disability. A 5-year-old who does not walk or talk obviously has a disability. The inability of an adult to read is not a reading disability if she or he has not had instruction that leads most people to read. The inability of a seeing person to see well in the dark is not a disability, but the inability of a blind person to see well with sufficient light is a disability. The inability of the typical adult male to lift 400 pounds is not a disability because most adult males are not expected to be able to lift such weight. The inability of the typical 70-year-old to run 10 miles is not considered a disability, although the inability to walk at age 70 is. The point is simply that disability is a significant difference from what we expect most people to be able to do, given their age, opportunities, and instruction.

All Exceptionalities Represent Continuous Distributions

Another important point about all exceptionalities, whether disabilities or giftedness, is that they represent continuous distributions. This means that they all vary from a lot to a little, with very fine gradations possible. Moreover, *exceptional* fades into *typical* or *normal* without a distinction that is crystal clear. True, there are the obvious cases. But many cases are not obvious because an individual is on the borderline and it is not really clear on which side of a line (exceptional or not exceptional; mild or moderate; moderate or severe) he or she belongs. But failure to acknowledge that we need a line and have to struggle with which side some cases are on results, predictably, in denial of exceptionality and denial of special services. Lines, like the one defining poverty, abuse, adolescence, or senior citizen, are important. Refusal to draw such lines merely ensures that conditions or problems will either be denied or not addressed effectively.

Most Disabilities are Mild

A third important point is that most disabilities are mild, not severe. The largest category of students receiving special education is that of learning disabilities. In fact, more than half of all students receiving special education today are identified as learning disabled. Relatively few students receiving special education are identified as having severe or multiple disabilities. Severe mental retardation, autism, deafness, and blindness are comparatively rare disabilities, and deaf-blindness is extremely rare. So it is common for special educators to speak of *high incidence* and *low incidence* disabilities. High incidence refers to the disabilities most commonly identified, which include learning disabilities, speech-language disorders, mild mental retardation, and emotional disturbance. The other disability categories are generally considered low-incidence, simply because they are relatively seldom encountered. In the light of our discussion in Chapter 2, you might rightly conclude that low incidence disabilities are those that relevant measurement indicates are even further from the mean—even further out under the left tail of the curve—than high incidence disabilities. But they may also be syndromes or combinations of disabilities that are rare.

Mental Retardation

Definition

Mental retardation (MR) includes significantly below average intellectual ability. However, it is not defined just by low intellectual ability (which is estimated with a standardized test of intelligence to obtain an "intelligence quotient" or IQ). MR also refers to substantial limitations in ability to function in everyday circumstances. It involves impairments in some of the following skill areas: communication, self-care, self-direction, social skills, home health and safety, use of community agencies and services, leisure activities (e.g., recreation), work, and functional academics. In other words, MR is defined by both low intellectual ability *and* limitations in skills required for independent living (often called *adaptive* skills or adaptive behavior). Adaptive behavior is usually measured by a standardized rating scale, for which parents, teachers, or others are asked to rate the individual's performance on a variety of tasks based on their observations.

The cut-off score or criterion for both IQ and adaptive behavior are arbitrary—that is, they can be changed, moved up or down, at will. No definition of MR is free of criticism. However, nearly everyone agrees that some people need extra support in everyday functioning, and that among the reasons for such special needs are low intellectual ability and limited adaptive skills. In fact, the American Association on Mental Retardation (AAMR) refers to four levels of support needed: intermittent, limited, extensive, and pervasive. That is, some people with MR need only occasional support; others need consistent but circumscribed or limited support. For some, the supports needed are extensive, involving nearly every type of activity; pervasive support is demanded for some, as they have very minimal ability to meet the demands of everyday living. Some within AAMR believe that levels of support should replace levels of mild, moderate, severe, and profound MR, and the even older designations of "educable" (able to learn functional academic skills), "trainable" (not able to learn academics, but able to learn self-care skills), and "custodial" (not able to learn basic self-care skills).

We caution here that all of the *levels* or *degrees* of MR, not just the general definition, are somewhat arbitrary. Perhaps the most important reason for the arbitrariness or ambiguity in the definition and the levels is that intelligence and adaptive skills are continuously distributed. Recall our discussion of measurement and continuous distributions in the last chapter and our previous comment about how all exceptionalities are continuous distributions. MR, like all continuous distributions (including intelligence and adaptive skills), varies from a lot to a little, with very fine gradations possible. So the "cut point" where MR begins or where the level of "intermittent" support turns to "limited" support (or "moderate" turns to "severe," or "educable" turns to "trainable," etc.) is unavoidably arbitrary and fuzzy. They (both the general definition and a degree or level) can be changed at will. Moreover, there are and always will be individuals on the border of any criterion we set. Finally, some cases are relatively clear (for example, it is unlikely that anyone would argue that the individual has MR or that the level of support required is "pervasive"), but other cases are not crystal clear, and cogent arguments can be made either way (e.g., the child *does* or *does not* have MR). And because the human beings who make the decisions about MR and all of the algorithms (mathematical formula for determining MR) are less than perfect, sometimes individuals are misidentified (either mistakenly considered to have MR or overlooked and not identified as having MR when they actually have it). We need to be able to accept the ambiguity of *not* having a gold standard (i.e., not having a definitive criterion). In other words, there always may be reasonable disagreement on close cases.

Why Special Education May Be Needed

It isn't difficult for most people to see why students with more severe MR (those who need extensive or pervasive support) need special education. They clearly have educational needs that differ significantly from the educational needs of most students. They are very unlikely to become proficient at the academic skills that most children master before high school, even with the most intensive and persistent instruction. They need a curriculum focusing on the adaptive skills that will allow them to become as independent as possible, although it is clear that they will need lots of support for the rest of their lives. They are extremely unlikely to receive such instruction from general education teachers.

However, for students with milder levels of MR (those needing only intermittent or limited support) there are often arguments about what disability the individual has and what should be done to accommodate him or her. Most of the students who have a mild level of MR will need special instruction if they are to learn basic academics and be prepared for the world of work. Without such special education, it is virtually certain that they will fail to attain the level of academic competence they could otherwise and that they will fail to learn the skills they will need for successful employment and everyday living.

Learning Disability

Definition

Students with one or more learning disability (LD) were at one time called *minimally brain injured, slow learner, dyslexic,* or *perceptually disabled.* LD has been used as the designation for this type of exceptionality since the 1960s. The category is very controversial, and some may argue that it is a phantom category (does not actually exist), that the identification of LD is fatally flawed, or that far too many students in the United States are considered to have a LD. Our own view is that LD does exist and that estimates of its over-identification are overblown—that most of the students identified as having LD really do have it.

The definition and identification of LD are matters of great debate. For years, the standard method of determining whether a student had LD relied on the measurement of a discrepancy between achievement in one or more academic areas (usually measured by means of a standardized achievement test) and ability (as measured by a standardized intelligence test). In other words, a student was identified as having LD when he or she failed to learn at the expected level in a particular academic area.[5] More recently, there has been a call to focus, instead, on the student's inability to respond successfully to sound instruction delivered in the general education classroom.[6] In other words, a student would be identified as having LD if he or she does not progress at the same rate and level as his or her peers when taught using proper instruction (validated by research as effective).

Regardless of which method one uses to identify LD, we are talking about a situation in which the student's performance in a given area is inconsistent with the expectations we have based on other information. That is, there is no reasonable explanation (like MR, mental illness, economic disadvantage, poor teaching, or impaired vision or hearing) for the student's failure to learn. Whether LD is seen as a discrepancy between tested intelligence and educational achievement or a lack of responsiveness to instruction, the fact is that his or her learning is below expectations, and there seems to be no explanation for this other than a possible brain dysfunction.

Like MR, LD can range from very severe to nearly normal. In fact, LD fades into "normal" or "typical" like any other exceptionality, and its definition is, therefore, an arbitrary matter, and identification of LD requires informed judgment.

Why Special Education May Be Needed

Students with LD fail, by definition, with the instruction offered in general education. If they respond well to instruction that is successful with most students and learn as expected of typical students, then they do not have a learning disability. If they do not receive special education, then it is highly predictable that students with LD will continue to fail.

Some students with LD can be taught in general education classes if their teachers have special training. However, those with the most severe levels of LD may need special teaching in a special setting aside from the general classroom. The reason they may need such special education is that they have very special, persistent difficulties in learning that do not and will not respond to the instruction offered to most students or instruction that is only slightly different or slightly adapted to special needs.[7]

Attention Deficit-Hyperactivity Disorder

Definition

A great deal of controversy has surrounded most aspects of attention deficit-hyperactivity disorder (ADHD). The prevailing opinion of experts in the field is that ADHD is a problem of inhibiting behavior. Individuals with ADHD cannot ignore things that most people can. They are easily distracted and cannot focus their attention. They may know the proper way to behave but be unable to engage in socially appropriate behavior. They thus often seem "scattered," unfocused, and socially obtuse or maddening because they interrupt or misinterpret others' conversations or activities, forget what most people can remember, or otherwise frustrate and anger others by their fidgeting or distractibility.

Not all people with ADHD are hyperactive. That is, they do not all engage in high levels of seemingly meaningless activity. However, the common thread of

ADHD is inability to focus and inability to inhibit certain behaviors that are necessary to normal functioning in our society.

ADHD can range from mild to severe. It can also be episodic—be more evident sometimes than others, occur in waves or spells. Thus an individual with ADHD may function well sometimes or in some circumstances, but at other times have extraordinary difficulty. The episodic nature of ADHD confuses some people and convinces them that the individual with ADHD *could* focus attention, *could* behave appropriately but simply *chooses* not to. However, the person with ADHD really does not make a conscious choice to behave inappropriately. The exceptionality is a matter of neurological dysfunction that requires special training and very possibly medication.

Why Special Education May Be Needed

Most students with ADHD drive teachers, not just themselves and their families, to distraction. They are difficult to manage and teach in a large group. Some excellent teachers, including some general educators with training in what to do for such students, can help such students be successful. However, where and how the instruction of a student with ADHD needs to be atypical depends on the nature and degree of the ADHD. Medications may be helpful to some students, but nearly all students with ADHD require special management and instruction that parents and teachers must be trained to provide.

Emotional or Behavioral Disorder

Definition

Emotional or behavioral disorder (EBD) may be even harder to define crisply than MR, LD, or ADHD. In federal laws and regulations, EBD is often referred to as *emotional disturbance.* The terminology is somewhat confusing, but in general this exceptionality refers to behavior that persistently and significantly disturbs adults and peers. The fact that adults and peers are upset by the behavior does not mean that the problem is merely one of their needing to learn to tolerate it. Students with EBD are outliers in the distribution of social skills and adaptive behavior. Their offensiveness to others may be due to their disregard of social norms, but often this offensiveness is also problematic because it is very discrepant from developmental norms. Their behavior, if uncorrected, means that they will likely have increasing problems in getting along with others. Their emotional problems, if inadequately addressed, mean that they will be hampered not only in interpersonal relationships but also in self-understanding, self-acceptance, and happiness.

There are many different ways to be emotionally disturbed, many different types of emotional and behavioral disorders. Behavior may vary along the dimensions of *externalizing* (acting out, aggression) or *internalizing* (acting in, depression) or both, with many variations being possible.[8]

Some of the students with EBD have conditions usually classified as mental illness, such as schizophrenia or bipolar disorder (formerly called manic depression, signifying mood swings from unnatural elation and over-activity to depression), obsessions, compulsions, extreme anxiety, and so on. In short, EBD may be defined by behavior or emotional responses in school so different from those of other students the same age, and from cultural or ethnic expectations, that they adversely affect educational performance, including academic, social, vocational, or personal skills. EBD is more than a temporary, expected response to stressful events. It is exhibited in multiple settings (e.g., school and home). It is persistent, not temporary. It can coexist with other disabilities. It includes disorders of thinking (e.g., schizophrenia), affect, anxiety, conduct, or adjustment.[9]

Why Special Education May Be Needed

Students with EBD often do not respond to a school and classroom structure that is conducive to the development of most students. They may require far more teacher monitoring and direction than typical students. They may need a smaller school or classroom to be able to function well. They may need more precise and remedial instruction in academic areas, direct training in social skills, or other adaptations that are extremely difficult to make in a regular classroom. They may be so disruptive in a regular classroom that they take an inordinate amount of the teacher's time and energy and interfere with the progress of other students. Or they may be so unresponsive in a regular class that it is impossible to instruct them with typical students.

Communication Disorder

Definition

Disorders of communication can involve speech or language or both. Speech refers to making sounds and putting them together properly so that one can be understood by a listener. Language refers to sending and receiving ideas, comprehending and using symbols, the communication of meaning.

Speech includes articulation (making speech sounds), fluency (the rhythm and flow of speech), and voice. Speech therapists may work on articulation to make a student more understandable. They may work on fluency to help someone overcome or adapt to stuttering. They may work on voice to help a person use pitch, loudness, and pleasing vocal quality to be more socially acceptable or to avoid causing problems with laryngitis or other complications.

Language involves the form, content, and social uses of speech (or other language, such as signing or computer-generated speech). Language therapists may help a student understand and use grammar appropriately, understand the appropriate content of speech, and use language appropriately and effectively in social circumstances.

There are many variations in communication that are not disorders. Many of these variations are related to the individual's social or cultural identity. It is important not to confuse dialects and accents, for example, with speech or language disorders. A communication disorder hampers communication, causes embarrassment to the speaker, or draws unnecessary attention within a communication community. It is a difference from expected communication in the individual's usual social context.

Sometimes communication disorders occur without other disabilities. However, communication disorders also often occur along with other disabilities. In fact, communication disorders are a prominent feature of some other disabilities, such as autism and mental retardation. Some special educators believe that communication disorders are the underlying problem in learning disabilities or emotional and behavioral disorders.

Why Special Education May Be Needed

Communication disorders are among the most complex exceptionalities. It is not feasible to teach all classroom teachers everything they need to know about how to identify, assess, and correct all disorders of communication. True, much can be done by regular classroom teachers to address communication problems, particularly when they are advised by a speech-language specialist. However, some of the work for some students needs to be done by a specialist, occasionally in a different environment than the typical classroom.

Also, some individuals need to use a communication system other than speech, either because they do not hear speech or because they have physical disabilities that prevent them from using their vocal mechanism to produce speech. These students may need augmentative or alternative communication systems or devices. They may be able to use these systems or devices in typical social contexts once they are equipped with them, but a specialist may be required to evaluate what the individual needs and provide initial training in its use.

Deafness

Definition

Hearing acuity can be measured fairly precisely. It is possible to find out through testing (usually by a specialist in hearing, an audiologist) what sound frequencies (pitches) a person can hear at a given level of intensity or loudness. As is true for most human traits, hearing acuity is a continuous distribution. One's hearing can be very sharp, about average (or typical), a little below average, or way below normal. For educational purposes, a person who is hard-of-hearing needs a hearing aid to make use of oral language. For educational purposes, someone who is deaf does not have enough residual hearing to process oral language, even with a hearing aid.

Why Special Education May Be Needed

Normal development of oral language depends on hearing. True, effective communication is possible without speech—through signing (manual communication). It is also true that some teachers in regular classrooms may learn some signs, particularly if a deaf student is in the classroom. However, most of the world is hearing, and most of the world uses oral language for communication. And most regular classroom teachers and their students do not become proficient enough in signing to make the classroom a communication-rich environment, which it needs to be if the student is to thrive academically and socially.

Thus, for many deaf students, a special classroom or school in which nearly *all* communication is manual or supplemented by signing is essential to meet their academic and social needs. Learning manual communication is, essentially, like learning another language, and one does not become proficient in teaching and using it in the typical oral social context. Having learned to sign does not mean that a student is now easily accommodated in a regular classroom. Communication, including social exchanges, depends on having a language community—people who speak your language fluently. Most people are not fluent and are not likely to become fluent in signing. Hence, students who are deaf and placed in regular classrooms are very likely to remain socially and linguistically isolated. This may be why more than 15 percent of deaf students are educated in separate schools and another 25 percent are taught primarily outside regular classes.[10] Many deaf people and educators of the deaf see special schools as critical to the success of deaf students. For example,

> Rachel Bavister, who taught deaf students at the [Virginia School for the Deaf] for 30 years, describes it as an incubator for independence, sheltering students just long enough to teach them how to get along in the world. Among her former students, she said, are a professor of clinical psychology and an accountant.
>
> "We have deaf staff and staff who communicate, so our kids have absolutely no excuse not to grow up to be citizens, hold a job and contribute," Bavister, who is deaf, said in a written interview.[11]

Vision Impairment and Blindness

Definition

Visual acuity can be measured fairly precisely. It is possible to find out through testing (usually by a vision specialist, an ophthalmologist or optometrist) how acute a person's vision is and what level of correction is necessary for specific purposes, such as driving, reading, or walking about. As is true for most human traits, visual acuity is a continuous distribution. Someone's vision can be very sharp, about average (or typical), a little below average, or way below normal. For educational purposes, a person with low vision needs extraordinary corrective lenses, lighting, or large print. For educational purposes, someone who is blind cannot use print and must learn Braille for reading and writing. They must also learn orientation and mobility skills to be independent.

Why Special Education May Be Needed

Most teachers can, with consultation, learn how to accommodate students with low vision in their regular classrooms. Some regular classroom teachers can accommodate students with blindness *if the students have previously learned Braille and orientation and mobility skills.*

Children who are blind can interact socially in ways that children who are deaf cannot because they have oral language. However, their independence and academic progress are likely to be stymied unless and until they become proficient in reading and writing Braille and in learning how to orient themselves to a physical environment and get around in it. Braille, orientation, and mobility are skills not likely to be learned without instruction by specialists in special classes or schools.

Physical Disability

Definition

Physical disabilities involve a very wide range of injuries, diseases, and chronic conditions that limit a person's ability to perform everyday activities. They include such conditions as cerebral palsy, seizure disorders, cystic fibrosis, asthma, limb anomalies, and other diseases and conditions too numerous to catalog. The main point is that because of some physical condition the individual cannot engage in typical activities or do them in the normal way. Some use wheelchairs or prostheses (artificial body parts). Some use adaptive devices (special equipment to help them accomplish typical tasks).

Physical disabilities may involve any organ system. For example, they may involve the brain or spinal column, bones, muscles, or organs of respiration, digestion, or circulation. And some disabilities involve multiple organ systems.

Physical disabilities also may be episodic or progressive, acute or chronic. Episodic disabilities come and go; those that are progressive get steadily worse. Acute disabilities are a crisis, from which a person may recover; those that are always present, at least at some level, are chronic.

Why Special Education May Be Needed

Many children with physical disabilities need little or no special education, as they can be relatively easily accommodated in a regular classroom. However, some need a protective or specialized environment, at least for a time, which is not feasible in a regular classroom. Some are hospitalized frequently and require instruction in the hospital or at home if they are to keep up with their age peers academically.

Additionally, special education may be needed because children with physical disabilities may also have intellectual, sensory, or behavioral problems. Although most students with physical disabilities do not have other disabilities, those with some physical disabilities (e.g., cerebral palsy and seizure disorders) are more likely than physically normal students to have conditions such as learning disabilities and mental retardation.

Autistic Spectrum Disorder

Definition

Autism became a separate category of disability under the Individuals with Disabilities Education Act (IDEA) in 1990. It is now typically discussed under a broader term, "autistic spectrum disorder." Autistic spectrum disorder implies a qualitative impairment of social interaction and communication. It also is often characterized by restricted, repetitive, stereotyped patterns of behavior, interests, and activities. Besides autism, autistic spectrum disorder includes Asperger's disorder—much like autism, but milder and usually without significant delays in cognition and language. It also includes Rett's disorder (normal development for 5 months to 4 years, followed by regression and mental retardation) and childhood disintegrative disorder (normal development for at least 2 and up to 10 years, followed by significant loss of skills).

Autism is best thought of as a spectrum of disorders that may vary in severity, age of onset, and combination with other disorders (e.g., mental retardation, specific language delay). No single behavior is typical of all cases of autism, and no single behavior automatically excludes a child from the category of autistic spectrum disorder. Autistic spectrum disorder is a brain dysfunction, but no one knows exactly how the brain is affected or why the disorder occurs.

Why Special Education May Be Needed

Autistic spectrum disorder may require special education for the same reasons we have given in our discussion of mental retardation, emotional or behavioral disorder, and communication disorder. That is, depending on the individual student, special education may be necessary to address the student's extraordinary cognitive, social, and/or communication needs. Some students with autistic spectrum disorder will be able to function acceptably without special education, but many will not.

Traumatic Brain Injury

Definition

Like autism, traumatic brain injury (TBI) became a separate category of disability under IDEA in 1990. TBI is brain damage acquired by trauma after a period of normal neurological development. Commonly accepted definitions of TBI specify that (1) the injury to the brain is caused by an external force, (2) it is not caused by a degenerative or congenital condition, (3) it results in a diminished or altered state of consciousness, and (4) it causes neurological or neurobehavioral dysfunction. Most definitions also specify that the injury is followed by impairments in abilities required for school learning and everyday functioning.

TBI has two subcategories of injury: open and closed. Open head injuries involve a penetrating head wound from such causes as a fall, gunshot, assault, vehicular accident, or surgery. In closed head injuries, there is no open head wound but brain damage is caused by internal compression, stretching, or other shearing motion of neural tissues within the head, such as might result from violent shaking of a child by an adult.

Why Special Education May Be Needed

TBI presents unique educational problems that often have been poorly understood and mismanaged. The possible effects of TBI include a long list of learning and psychosocial problems, including language problems, thinking problems, and emotional or behavioral problems. TBI is often "invisible." Like a learning disability, it is not something that someone is likely to notice about a person at first. In some cases, a person with TBI has paralysis or slurred speech or some other indicator of brain damage that is quickly apparent, but in many cases the person with TBI looks just like everyone else and appears at first to behave normally. However, students with TBI may need special education for problems in a variety of areas, including thinking, remembering, planning, interpreting and displaying emotions, relearning skills that have been lost, and so on. Many students with TBI simply cannot resume their former lives and be successful without extraordinary help from teachers.

Deaf-Blindness and Other Severe and Multiple Disabilities

Definition

Without going into the technicalities of definitions, we note that some students may be both deaf *and* blind or have multiple disabilities—two or more disabilities, sometimes severe (e.g., mental retardation *and* physical disabilities; emotional *and* communication disorders; deafness, mental retardation, seizures, *and* emotional disturbance). No exceptionality immunizes an individual against others. In fact, some disabilities (e.g., cerebral palsy) usually are accompanied by others as well.

However, multiple disabilities are relatively rare—low incidence. They usually involve greater severity (of mental retardation, for example) or syndromes that are known to involve brain injury (e.g., traumatic brain injury, which usually has multiple effects) and brain dysfunction (e.g., autism or autistic spectrum disorder, which is a brain problem of unknown nature and origin).

Why Special Education May Be Needed

Students with deaf-blindness and other severe or multiple disabilities have unusually complex educational needs. For most people it is not difficult to understand why special education is required for deaf-blind or autistic students. Without highly specialized, persistent, carefully modulated instruction, these students are very unlikely to learn the academic, social, and adaptive skills required for independent living.

Giftedness and Special Talents

Definition

The definition of giftedness is quite controversial. In part, this is true because giftedness is often thought to be defined by IQ, and intelligence testing is controversial. One of the big controversies involves whether a person has a general intelligence or more specific kinds of intelligence, whether there are multiple intelligences. Should aspects of intelligence be lumped together or split apart?

But beyond IQ or intelligence, the controversy is about whether we should be able to anticipate giftedness or identify it after the fact. Anticipation means making a guess, usually based on test scores or teachers' judgments or both, that a student is or has the potential to be gifted. Identification after the fact means that educators wait until the student actually has demonstrated achievement way beyond that of typical students his or her age.

Besides controversy about when or how to identify gifted and talented students, there is disagreement about just what should be measured or included in gifts and talents. Most would include performance in academic areas and the arts. But should giftedness or talents include athletics? Social leadership? Moral perception? Other personal qualities?

Whatever is included or measured, another issue is how much above average a person must be to be considered gifted or talented and, of course, just who should comprise the comparison group? Should the student be in the highest performing 10 percent, 5 percent, 1 percent, or what percent? Should the student be compared to others in the nation, state, school district, school, or some other group? Should the student be compared to all students in an attendance area or only to those of his or her own gender, social class, or ethnic group?

We do not have definitive answers to these questions, but it seems clear to us that students who are gifted or talented stand out clearly from the typical in their performance, motivation, and commitment to a particular activity that is highly valued in our society.

Why Special Education May Be Needed

Because ability or performance in any area is continuously distributed, the identification of a cut-point for triggering special education is arbitrary and open to change. Many people in our society do not have much sympathy for gifted students and may, in fact, resent them or assume that if they're so smart they can take care of themselves. However, without access to a curriculum that is challenging to them—whether it is in math, science, music, or any other area of performance—they are likely to be bored and achieve far less than they could otherwise.

Federal law has never mandated special education for gifted students as it has for students with disabilities, perhaps reflecting our society's antipathy toward giftedness. Certain groups of gifted students have been particularly neglected, including females, students with disabilities, and students from some cultural and ethnic minorities. Regardless of the personal identification of students with special gifts or talents, it is predictable that the greater the discrepancy between their abilities and those of their typical peers, the less likely that their educational needs will be met without special education.

Why Some Exceptional Students Do Not Need Special Education

Not every exceptionality requires special education because (a) some disabilities, such as some physical limitations, are unrelated to education or the student may be well taught and well managed by a good general education teacher and (b) disabilities, even those related to education, can be so mild or transitory that special education is unnecessary. Special education is for those students who are significantly, persistently at the fringes of educational performance (are significant outliers in a statistical distribution) and will succeed in school only if they receive instruction that most students do not get and cannot be expected to get.

Why Prevention of Disabilities
Is Often Not Practiced

Nearly everybody agrees with prevention in principle, but few are willing to implement preventive practices. The reasons are many, and have been discussed elsewhere.[12] Given attitudes toward special education, however, the resistance to prevention is probably understandable.

Why would people resist preventing disabilities? First, prevention can be practiced at one of three levels, two of which cannot be practiced without labeling. *Primary* prevention means doing the same thing for everyone so that a problem simply does not occur. *Secondary* prevention means taking action after a problem occurs to prevent it from getting worse and to overcome it if you can. *Tertiary* prevention means managing a problem so that complications do not occur and learning to cope with it the best way possible. For primary prevention, no label is necessary, as everyone is treated the same. But for secondary and tertiary prevention, a label of some kind—talking about the problem, using a word for it—is unavoidable. We cannot prevent problems we do not talk about, talking about them involves labels, and once a problem has occurred we must talk about a particular individual as having the problem.

Second, prevention requires anticipation. We cannot prevent what we do not anticipate (i.e., after something happens, it is too late to prevent it). Many people are loath to anticipate a disability or complications of it, preferring to deal with problems only after the fact and believing that anticipation will somehow cause a problem to occur. In other words, they believe that merely expecting a problem to occur will almost automatically lead to its occurrence. We do not doubt that expectations can influence performance, but we do think that such occurrences are relatively uncommon— uncommon enough that it should not deter us from seeking to anticipate disabilities.

Third, prevention would require serving more students, serving them at younger ages and earlier in their difficulties, and spending more money. All of these are absolute necessities if prevention is to be made a reality, but all are anathema to those who feel special education already serves too many students, costs too much, and is too quickly deemed as necessary.

Fourth, prevention requires having more individuals in the "borderline" category. That is, it is a mathematical certainty that if problems are caught earlier we will (a) serve a larger number of individuals and (b) have uncertainty about a greater number of students. If you think about a continuous distribution of performance, you will understand why this is true. Imagine moving a line further from the left tail of a distribution and closer to the mean or average. Understanding that the higher the point on the curve the greater the number of individuals, it is absolutely certain that *moving toward less extreme problems or disabilities means that the number of individuals involved is greater and the number who are right on or very near the line will be greater, too.* Review Figure 2.1 and you will see what we mean. Any line drawn closer to the central tendency (mean, median, and mode) includes a greater number of individuals than does a line drawn further from the central tendency. Many people think it is important to have certain knowledge of whether a child does or does not have a disability, and whether he or she should or should not have special services. However, prevention requires taking action without absolute certainty that a child has or will have a disability.

Fifth, prevention requires something extra, not just what we have in place now. Even primary prevention demands that something be added or changed, which costs money and requires extra effort. Secondary and tertiary prevention require even more in the way of extras. What should the extra educational things be called? If they are called special education, some people will object, as special education is considered undesirable.

Not all disabilities can be prevented, but many could be prevented from ever occurring (e.g., through better health and safety practices, genetic counseling, better education, better child rearing). Many could be addressed early, preventing them from getting worse or reversing them and improving the long-term prognosis. Unwillingness to take preventive action inevitably increases the monetary and human costs, although it does save money in the short term and allows people to avoid confronting unwelcome realities for a while. As a society, we respond to crises once they have occurred, but we do not respond very well to anticipation of them or to the things we can see leading up to them.

Summary

Students may need special education for a variety of reasons. Chief among these reasons are special difficulties in thinking (cognition); learning an academic subject or subjects (achievement not consistent with cognitive ability); focusing and sustaining attention or being reasonably still and accessible to teaching; recognizing and controlling emotions or behavior; communicating through speech, hearing, seeing, moving or maintaining physical well-being, or severe disabilities or multiple areas of disability (i.e., extreme disabilities or several disabilities in combination). Students may also need special education because they have extraordinary abilities. The common categorical designations of these exceptionalities are mental retardation, learning disabilities, attention deficit-hyperactivity disorder, emotional and behavioral disorders, communication disorders, hearing impairment and deafness, vision problems and blindness, physical disabilities, autistic spectrum disorder, traumatic brain injury, multiple and severe disabilities, and giftedness and talentedness. These disabilities and extraordinary abilities may occur in many combinations. Many of the students in each of these categories need special education, although some do not. Prevention of disabilities seems like a good principle, but efforts to put prevention into practice meet with substantial resistance.

B O X **3.1**

Case in Point

The educators in Jimmy's school see his lag in reading ability as obvious, and it also has been confirmed by testing. The evidence suggests that Jimmy does not have a general problem in thinking well, because when he is *told* things he makes good sense of them. What seems to cause him particular problems is decoding written language (i.e., being able to automatically, fluently turn letters and words into their associated sounds). So, for the past year he has received special education instruction for one hour each day in a resource room program. The rest of the time he has been in his regular class. When his regular class has reading, he has gone to the resource room for special instruction in how to associate letters and written words with sounds.

REFERENCE NOTES

1. Hallahan & Kauffman (2003, p. 4).
2. Bateman & Linden (1998).
3. Hall (2002).
4. Hallahan & Kauffman (2003).
5. See Kavale (2002).
6. See Gresham (2002); Vaughn & Fuchs (2003).
7. See Hallahan, Lloyd, Kauffman, Weiss, & Martinez (2005).
8. See Kauffman (2005a) for detailed description, examples, and discussion.
9. See Forness & Knitzer (1992) for discussion of the definition of the Mental Health and Special Education Coalition, a coalition of more than 30 organizations. See Kauffman (2005a) for detailed discussion of definition.
10. U.S. Department of Education (2002).
11. Helderman (2003, p. B7).
12. Kauffman (1999, 2003, 2005a, 2005b, in press b).

4 The Nature of Special Education

What is special about special education? What makes it different from good general education, or from the good teaching of *any* teacher? The answer isn't simple. We might be tempted to think that special and general education are the same if they're both good. However, they are not the same. Teaching exceptional learners well requires substantially greater precision and persistence along some of the dimensions of instruction—pacing, number of trials, structure, reinforcement, and so on. Just as teaching general education students requires great skill in teaching typical students in larger groups, special education requires great skill in teaching smaller groups of those who are atypical and delivering education to exceptional learners more precisely than is possible in general education.[1]

In this chapter we discuss the dimensions of education that make—or at least *could and should* make—special education different from general education. We conclude the chapter with the observation that special education's bottom line is effective instruction of learners at the extremes of a distribution of performance.

How Special Education Is—or Can Be—Special

Special education is not always truly special. Like everything else, it is sometimes poorly practiced. Nevertheless, special education can be, should be, and at least sometimes is truly special—different from the typical, something general education cannot be. One special education teacher described how his teaching of students with severe developmental delays is necessarily different from general education for his students:

> *Teaching to assess:* Virtually all lessons with severely delayed students contain probing to see where weaknesses and strengths are. The frequency and precision of this probing are not necessary or productive for typical learners. They would be a waste of time.

> *Micro Task Analysis:* Steps to learning frequently have to be broken down into sub-segments that most people wouldn't even see as discreet steps. Such small steps are unnecessary in general education and would slow the progress of typical students.

47

Minimizing Stimulus Error: Learning materials must be screened for extraneous elements to ensure that students are focusing on the right thing. Materials typically used in general education would be massively confusing or distracting for special education students. Elimination of all distracting elements isn't necessary for typical students.[2]

Special education is truly special when it is more precise and more tightly controlled than general education can be. True, it must be focused on *educating,* not merely placing a student in a different class. Special education has its most significant effect when the *education* of students is the foremost concern, as scholars Kenneth Kavale and Steven Forness have shown.[3]

Special education is not different from general education in its basic operations, but it is different in the application of these operations. It is different from general education along specific dimensions that we discuss further:

- Pacing or Rate
- Intensity
- Relentlessness
- Structure
- Reinforcement
- Pupil:Teacher Ratio
- Curriculum
- Monitoring or Assessment

Of course, the dimensions of teaching are continuously distributed. (You may recall from Chapter 2 that in a continuous distribution what is measured can vary from a little to a lot, with fine gradations possible.) All of the dimensions of teaching range from a little to a lot, with very fine gradations possible. Thus the distinction between general and special education is somewhat "fuzzy," a somewhat arbitrary distinction. This doesn't mean that special education is just imaginary any more than exceptionalities are imaginary because they can be very mild or difficult to distinguish from typical development. It means that as students can "sort of" have an exceptionality, it is possible to "sort of" have special education—education that is on the border between general and special. Where to draw the line between general and special is a good question. Refusal to draw a line, though, means that a critically important distinction won't be made, and therefore many students will be poorly served. They won't get the instruction they need if we presume that special education doesn't really exist or can't be distinguished from good general education.

We can describe the dimensions of teaching and describe how special education differs from the more general. The distinction is a matter of degree. The degree of difference on the dimensions of teaching matters, as does the degree of difference in student characteristics defining exceptionality.

Pacing or Rate

Rate of instruction refers to two things: (a) the pace with which a given lesson proceeds (i.e., the speed with which tasks are presented and responses demanded) and (b) the pace with which a student is led through a body of knowledge (i.e., the speed with which the teacher builds concepts, discriminations, or competencies). Most students learn well with a typical pace of both types. Some students learn little or nothing unless the teacher alters the pace significantly.

Good instruction is paced at a proper rate for the child's ability to learn whatever is being taught. All really good instruction is relatively fast-paced *for learners with particular characteristics.* That is, students are presented tasks at what, for them, is a rapid rate, and they are given frequent opportunities to respond. There is little "down time," when there is nothing to do. The pace is fast enough that the student does not get bored and is challenged, yet slow enough that the student can keep up.[4]

One way in which special education is different from general education is that it accommodates both the extremes of students' abilities to respond to instructional tasks and the interaction of instructional rate with content. That is, for some students, the pace at which tasks are presented and responses are demanded must be altered from the pace appropriate for typical learners. For some atypical students who have great difficulty in learning or responding, the tasks must be presented at a slower rate and the "wait time" that the teacher allows for responding must be longer than that desirable for typical students. For other atypical students who learn very quickly and easily, the rate must be faster than the appropriate speed for most students.

The optimum rate of instruction is not the same for all students. It may well be *about* the same for the great majority of students, but for those at the extremes or fringes of performance (either high or low), the rate may need to be altered significantly. If the rate is altered for all students, those who are typical suffer. If it is not altered, those at the extremes suffer. The only way to get the rate right is to make accommodations for those at the extremes by grouping them for instruction so that the rate of the lesson matches their abilities.

Thus, special educators must be acutely aware of pacing and know how to alter both the pace of presenting tasks and requiring responses and the rate or progress through a curriculum. The typical teacher is not taught to do this with great precision—to accommodate the extremes of learner characteristics—nor is the typical teacher able to make all of the necessary accommodations in the context of the regular classroom without jeopardizing the learning of either exceptional children or those who are typical.

Intensity

Most typical students should experience general education as being intensely demanding. Many do not. And many general education students are not given many hours of instruction or opportunities to respond. Part of many plans to reform general education include stepping up the intensity of instruction—increasing the hours that a specific skill (e.g., reading) is taught and increasing the frequency of students' responses to tasks. The school day or school year may be lengthened or the amount of homework may be increased.

Regardless of attempts to reform general education by increasing the intensity of instruction for all students, some exceptional children will need greater intensity than can be offered in the regular classroom if they are to perform as much like typical children as possible. They may need additional trials, more practice or review, a longer period of instruction, a more "fine-grained" curriculum (one with smaller steps or skills broken down further into components) than is appropriate for general education students, even those who are relatively low performers but do not have disabilities.

Other exceptional learners, namely those who are gifted or talented, will find the intensity of instruction appropriate for most students of their chronological age ridiculously low. That is, they learn so easily and rapidly that the intensity in instruction for most students, even if it is "jacked up," is only moderate or weak. These gifted students need something markedly different from the typical if they are to be challenged. They are unlikely to find appropriate challenges in a regular classroom. Usually, they must be grouped with others whose abilities are similar—either students who are chronologically older (i.e., they are accelerated or advanced through grades quicker than their typical age peers) or age peers with similarly extraordinary abilities.[5]

Relentlessness

All good teachers give their students repeated trials as needed, review material, and try to reach all of their students. But there comes a time when any good general education teacher moves on because most or all of the students have learned the concept or skill being taught. Sometimes, this means leaving low performers behind (i.e., they have not mastered the idea or skill; they have not become competent in the subject matter). It cannot be otherwise in general education, for otherwise the majority of students would be held back—they would not make the progress expected of typical students.

Special education teachers give learners with disabilities more trials, opportunities, attention, and instructional time. True, they may eventually decide that trying to teach a particular student a particular skill is fruitless and turn to teaching something else. However, the tenacity, persistence, and relentlessness of the special education teacher go beyond what can be offered in general education. The teacher may try a variety of instructional approaches that the general education teacher either does not know or cannot implement in the context of teaching a larger, general class of students.

Gifted students may find the review and repeated trials that are necessary for typical or slower learners to be a waste of their time. They can advance through material much faster than normal, learning skills and concepts with few trials and consolidating concepts with little review. If their needs are not accommodated, they become bored and find school a drag. Most teachers of typical students simply cannot provide the necessary accommodations for these students.[6]

Structure

Structure here refers to such things as (a) the explicitness of rules and expectations, (b) the regularity and predictability of routines, (c) the amount of teacher direction, (d) tolerance for misbehavior or its precursors, and (e) the immediacy, frequency, and explicitness of positive consequences for desirable behavior and negative consequences for unacceptable behavior. Most students do not need the "tightness" or high level of structure that is necessary for some students with disabilities. They do well without a highly and carefully structured learning environment, but many students with disabilities do not.

Typical children usually find a very high level of structure too confining and rigid, and rightfully so because they do not need it to behave and learn well. Some children with disabilities find such a high level of structure comforting, or they rely on it to get through the day without becoming upset or upsetting others. To be sure, a given classroom can have a somewhat differentiated structure for different students. But there are limits to the amount of differentiation that a teacher and students can manage. A given environment can no more be structured to be appropriate for every possible student than a given commercial retail establishment can meet the needs and desires of every possible customer. Sometimes the need for structure that is very different from that appropriate for most students can only be provided in a separate setting. Special education teachers have special training in how to structure the learning environment for students who do not respond well to the structure of good general education classrooms.

Some students are highly skilled at structuring their own lives or environments. They seem to have a knack for directing themselves. They are exceptions, not the rule. Most need a lot of teacher guidance. Some need teachers to control them a great deal, even more than typical students. Getting the amount of structure right for students requires different environments for learning, and these cannot all be created in the same place at the same time.[7]

Reinforcement

Although negative consequences (punishment) that are expertly used may have an important role in teaching and child rearing, the key to a positive and supportive classroom environment—general or special—is positive reinforcement, that is, rewarding desirable behavior and performance.[8] The general education classroom often does not provide sufficient or effective reinforcement for the learning and appropriate behavior of children with disabilities.

Well-trained special education teachers are skilled in finding and using positive reinforcement to support the learning and behavior of students who have special difficulty in school. They know that the following characteristics of reinforcement are effective, and they modulate such reinforcement so that it is effective for the individual student: immediacy, frequency, enthusiasm, eye contact, description of precisely what is being reinforced, student anticipation of reward, and variety of reward.[9]

Pupil:Teacher Ratio

Special education can offer many of its instructional benefits and structure because the teacher is responsible for dramatically fewer students than is the general education teacher. Teaching special education is particularly labor-intensive—it demands more adults per child than does general education. This is the case because special education involves more intensive and relentless instruction and a higher degree of structure than does general education.

Although it is undoubtedly true that reducing class size in general education or having two teachers in classes with students who have disabilities may work in some cases, in other cases it is extremely unlikely that students will be well-taught except in a special setting. Special education is a service, not a place, but the place constrains the kind of services that can be offered. Regardless of the student's placement, special education requires a lower ratio of pupils to teachers so that appropriate instruction and structure can be offered. "Smaller group ratios increase the likelihood of academic success through student–teacher interactions, individualization of instruction, student on-task behavior, and teacher monitoring of student progress and feedback."[10]

Curriculum

Many exceptional students can successfully learn the tasks that most students learn, although particularly precise teaching (special education) may be required if they are to make good progress. However, the general education curriculum is either inappropriate or does not contain all of the subjects or features that some exceptional children need. For example, orientation and mobility skills and Braille for students who are blind may be critical for them, but hardly necessary or desirable for most students. Likewise, most students do not need and cannot be expected to receive the intensity of instruction in signing that is necessary for deaf students. And most students do not require the intensive, explicit instruction in social skills that some students with emotional or behavioral disorders should receive.[11]

Students with severe cognitive disabilities—severe mental retardation—may require intensive and explicit teaching in curriculum areas that most students would find demeaning—dressing, toileting, self-feeding, or chewing and swallowing, and other self-care or daily living skills. Some children with speech or language disabilities need instruction in how to make speech sounds or use language to communicate—skills that most children learn without explicit instruction in school.

In short, the general education curriculum may be appropriate for most students, even for most students with disabilities. However, some children with disabilities require curricula that are not needed by most students, or they may need additional curricula if they are to be able to understand and respond correctly to the standard curriculum. The "what" of teaching—curriculum—cannot be the same for all students, unless those with disabilities simply aren't considered or are excluded from school entirely.

Monitoring or Assessment

All good teachers check frequently on their students' progress. However, it isn't necessary or feasible to monitor and assess the performance of most students as frequently or closely as is required for teaching those with disabilities. Students with disabilities require closer, more careful monitoring than is typical, similar to the medical patients in intensive care, for example.

Good training of special education teachers includes instruction in how to monitor students' progress daily in the curriculum. This intense level of monitoring is not necessary for typical students, but it is essential for those with special problems in learning. Their progress is often slow, especially in the beginning of their special education, and both they and their teachers need to be aware of progress, even if it is slow. Students with learning problems need more frequent and accurate feedback than do those whose learning is typical.[12]

Special and general education have differed in another way related to monitoring or assessment since the enactment of the federal special education law in 1975 (now IDEA, the Individuals with Disabilities Education Act). The "paper trail" required in special education is greater than that required in general education. All teachers, in both special and general education, must prepare lesson plans and report on the testing and progress of their students. However, the documentation required of teachers is greater in special education than in general education. The "paper trail" is documentation that procedures have been followed, including a written, individualized education plan (IEP) for each child with a disability. Educators must be able to document that parents have been involved (or that they have at least had reasonable opportunities to be involved) and have agreed with the referral and assessment of their child, their child's identification as needing special education, and the plan for their child's education. It is not reasonable to expect such extensive documentation for children who do not have disabilities.

Special Education on a Continuum

Special education consists of an extraordinary response to exceptionality. It employs the same dimensions of instruction that all educators use, but it is more intensive, relentless, and goal-directed than general education is or can be.[13] It is different instruction—not different in the essential acts that comprise teaching but different in the degree to which they are used and the precision with which they are employed. Consequently, a reasonable question regarding the education of any student is this: Just how special is it, and in what ways is it different? The answer can range from "sort of special in structure" (for example) to "very special along all dimensions of instruction."

Just as not all students with disabilities need special education, not all students need education that is special to the same degree. The difficult task is matching the degree of specialness to the needs of the student. Our view is that educators and parents very often underestimate the degree of specialness that is needed.

One of the difficulties in making special education truly special is the constraint that the place (physical location) of instruction puts on teaching. As we and others have noted elsewhere, it is not feasible to offer all types of instruction in the same place and at the same time.[14]

The degree of specialness possible seems to depend on three primary factors: (a) a teacher who has special training, is truly expert in implementing teaching procedures with extraordinary precision, (b) a small and relatively homogeneous group of students, and (c) a place in which teacher and students can work without undue interference or demands from others and in which their work does not compete with or impede the education of other students. Researcher and teacher educator Naomi Zigmond observed:

> Special education was once worth receiving; it could be again. In many schools, it is not now. Here is where practitioners, policymakers, advocates, and researchers in special education need to focus—on defining the nature of special education and the competencies of the teachers who will deliver it.[15]

At one time, prior to Public Law 94-142 (i.e., before 1975), the only option available for many students with disabilities was the self-contained classroom. Now, unfortunately, in many places the only option available for many students is the regular classroom. Even when full-time placement in the general education classroom is accompanied by having a special educator consult with, or even co-teach with the general educator, this can end up being a watered-down version of special education, a "sort of" special education. Movement toward full inclusion and consultation between special education and general education teachers rather than direct service to exceptional learners by special educators has had a high price. The focus on specialized instruction and the intention to train expert teachers in how to deliver such instruction have been largely lost. The improvement of special education—making it more reliably what it should be—awaits the rediscovery of such focus and intention.

Special Education's Bottom Line

Special education exists for the primary purpose of providing better instruction to students at the extremes of statistical distributions of achievement. Assessment, placement, and every other aspect of special education must serve the primary purpose of better instruction. If special education fails in this purpose, then it is derelict.

We do not mean to promote the view that special educators should focus on academics to the exclusion of everything else. Fostering or demanding such an exclusive focus would be perverse. Our point is simply that if special educators do not teach, then they have failed in their mission, regardless of how kind, sensitive, caring, or collaborative they might be. They could fail in their mission because all they do is teach academics and have no other concerns. But if they do not teach what their students need to learn, then all of the other things they may offer cannot make them competent special educators. Quoting researcher and teacher educator Naomi Zig-mond again:

> General educators cannot imagine focusing intensively on individual students to the extent that different instructional activities for different students are being implemented at the same time. This is simply impractical in a classroom of 25 to 35 students. More-over, special education's most basic article of faith, that instruction must be individual-ized to be truly effective, is rarely contemplated, let alone observed in most general education classrooms. Mainstream teachers must consider the good of the group and the extent to which the learning activities they present maintain classroom flow, orderliness, and cooperation. In addition, they generally formulate teaching plans that result in a pro-ductive learning environment for 90% or more of their students. General education set-tings are best for learning what most students need to learn.
>
> For many of the remaining 10% of students, however, a different orientation will probably be needed. These students need to learn something different because they are clearly not learning what everyone else is learning. Interventions that might be effective for this group of students require a considerable investment of time and effort, as well as extensive support.[16]

Summary

Although good general education is demanding, special education requires greater control and precision along several dimensions of instruction: pacing or rate, inten-sity, relentlessness, structure, reinforcement, pupil:teacher ratio, curriculum, and monitoring or assessment. Because all of these dimensions of teaching are continu-ous distributions (can vary from a little to a lot), education can differ in the degree of specialness. Ultimately, special education is only worthwhile if it means special in-struction for learners at the extremes of the distribution of performance.

BOX 4.1

Case in Point

In his resource room, Jimmy was taught by a special education teacher who knew that he needed reading instruction in decoding. The teacher had a low case load and was able to spend an entire hour each day working with Jimmy in a small group of students (five) sim-ilar in age and having similar reading problems. Jimmy was given instruction that focused on decoding, demanded frequent responses from him, provided immediate feedback, and gave him practice in using his skills in reading interesting material on his independent reading level. The teacher also maintained daily records of Jimmy's progress and kept his parents and regular teacher informed of how he was doing.

REFERENCE NOTES

1. Fuchs & Fuchs (1995); Kauffman (2002); Zigmond (2003). See also Heward (2003) for discussion of specious arguments about teaching.

2. Michael Gliona, personal communication, March, 2003.

3. Kavale & Forness (2000b).

4. For further discussion of pacing, see Berninger, Abbott, Vermeulen, Ogier, Brooksher, Zook, & Lemos (2002).

5. For further discussion of intensity of instruction see Foorman & Torgesen, (2001); Fuchs & Fuchs (2001); Moody, Vaughn, Hughes, & Fischer (2000).

6. For more discussion of relentless instruction see Horner, Sugai, & Horner (2000); Lewis, Colvin, & Sugai (2000).

7. For further discussion of structure see Boyda, Zentall, & Feiko (2002); Kauffman, Mostert, Trent, & Hallahan (2002); Swanson & Hoskyn (2001); Troia & Graham (2002).

8. Kauffman, Mostert, Trent, & Hallahan (2002).

9. For further discussion of reinforcement see Boyda et al. (2002); Horner, Sugai, Todd, & Lewis-Palmer (1999–2000); Kauffman, Mostert, Trent, & Hallahan (2002); Shores & Wehby (1999); Sutherland, Wehby, & Yoder (2002).

10. Vaughn, Linan-Thompson, Kouzekanani, Bryant, Dickson, & Blozis (2003), p. 301. For further discussion of pupil:teacher ratios see Foorman & Torgesen (2001); Rashotte, MacPhee, & Torgesen (2001); Vaughn, Gersten, & Chard (2000).

11. For further discussion of curriculum see Coyne, Kameenui, & Simmons (2001); Troia & Graham (2002).

12. For further discussion of monitoring see Espin, Busch, Shin, & Kruschwitz (2001); Fletcher, Foorman, & Boudousquie (2002); Walker & Sprague (1999).

13. Zigmond (1997; 2003). See Bateman (2004) for discussion of good teaching.

14. For example, see Kauffman (2002); Kauffman & Hallahan (1995, 1997, 2005); Kavale & Forness (2000a); Mock & Kauffman (2005).

15. Zigmond (1997, p. 389).

16. Zigmond (2003, p. 197).

5 Frequent Criticisms and Responses to Them

Special education is not beyond criticism. Certainly, it has its failures and faults. However, many critics misunderstand what special education is and can do. Special education has been criticized for many reasons. Here is a list of common complaints:

1. It is a failure because it does not produce good outcomes.
2. It costs too much.
3. It serves too many students, including many without disabilities.
4. Its identification procedures are unreliable; there is too much uncertainty about who needs it and who doesn't.
5. It stigmatizes students and ruins their identities.
6. It serves students for too many years and does not result in enough students losing their identity as having a disability.
7. It needs to be reconceptualized as a service, not a place.

In this chapter we first offer our responses to each of the criticisms we listed. Then we address some frequent questions about special education. We hope that you will be able to answer these questions based on your reading to this point, but we offer our own short answers as a reiteration of our discussion in previous chapters.

Responses to Criticisms

Outcomes Not Good

An important question about every kind of education is what happens to student outcomes when it "works" as it should. If special education works as it should, what is the result? The results or outcomes are usually measured by performance on standardized tests of academic achievement or on criteria said to measure "success," such as employment, earnings, and independent living without the use of social services.

Critics of special education are prone to compare outcomes for students with disabilities to those of students without disabilities—to suppose that if special education really works, then there will be no significant difference between the outcomes for students with disabilities and students without disabilities. This kind of comparison is unfair, misleading, and based on denial that many students have disabilities that directly affect academic achievement and social adaptation.

A more reasonable assessment of the outcomes of special education is what students with disabilities achieve *with* special education compared to what they achieve *without* it. Does special education help them do better than they would otherwise? No one knows very precisely how to answer this question for a very understandable reason: a rigorous scientific experiment—with students who are thought to *need* special education *randomly* assigned, half to receive special education and half not to receive special education—is impossible for legal and ethical reasons. The law demands that students who are identified as needing special education must receive it. Moreover, it would be ethically questionable to withhold special education from a student who is thought to need it. So experiments that would address the question (Does special education help; is it better than no special education?) are not possible. When critics of special education argue that the outcomes are not good, what logic and evidence do they use? Their logic has to rely on an unfair comparison—educational outcomes for students with disabilities compared to outcomes for students without disabilities. The evidence from fair comparisons to back up their criticism simply does not exist.

What logic and evidence do we use, then, to argue that the outcomes of special education are better than critics portray? Our logic is that the reasonable or valid comparison would be special education for students with disabilities versus no special education for students with disabilities. Although experimental data suggesting that special education is better than no special education do not exist (for reasons we've mentioned earlier), there are anecdotes and nonexperimental studies supporting the value of special education to students with disabilities. At least one nonexperimental study involving thousands of students and using sophisticated statistical procedures has found evidence that special education raises the achievement of students with disabilities over what it would have been without special education.[1] Furthermore, we can find many anecdotes to illustrate how the lives of students are typically made better, not worse, by their having received special education. Consider the personal story of Leonard E. Wright,

> who arrived [at the Staunton, Virginia, School for the Deaf] as a deaf 8-year-old in 1959, knowing no sign language and unable to communicate even with his parents. By Christmas, he was fluent. Wright graduated in 1970, went to college and became a teacher of deaf children.
>
> "The school allowed me the opportunity to be involved fully—literacy clubs, the drama clubs, Boy Scouts," he said through an interpreter. "They molded me into what I am."[2]

Or consider the following story told by a teacher of young children with mental retardation about changes in one of her students and the attitudes of this student's parents toward special education:

After a few weeks of Alice's placement in my room, the parents and I met again. They seemed much happier. "Alice enjoys coming to school now," they let me know. The dad, much to his credit, wished that he had not denied her services in the fall. "She feels so much better about herself now," he said.

Two years later, Alice's father and I talked about his reaction to the eligibility meeting (the one deciding that Alice qualified for my services). "There were so many people," he said, "and they were all saying that there was something terribly wrong with my daughter. I wondered who in the hell they were talking about! My pretty little girl is so loving and funny. How could they say she was retarded?"

"Does it matter what label they put on her? Isn't she still a pretty, funny, loving little girl?"

"Yeah," he laughed. "Except now she can read!"[3]

Costs Too Much

Special education, undeniably, costs more than general education. However, the costs of *not* having special education are even higher than the costs of having special education because children with disabilities typically do not learn how to become independent, productive citizens without it.

Special education requires extra teachers, either because a general education class in which students with disabilities are included has two teachers rather than one or because the pupil:teacher ratio is lower in special education than in general education. Special education costs are also higher than general education costs because of special transportation, curriculum materials, special equipment, and administration. However, in strictly economic terms, teaching children to become productive, independent citizens is a relative bargain.

Serves Too Many Students

When the Individuals with Disabilities Education Act was passed (in 1975, first known as the Education for All Handicapped Children Act, or Public Law 94-142) federal officials estimated that millions of children with disabilities were not receiving special education. Nowadays, a common complaint is that special education has grown too large and too many children have been identified as having disabilities and qualifying for special education. As a matter of fact, the number of children receiving special education grew rather dramatically from about 3.5 million in 1975 to over 5 million in the early twenty-first century.

Because special education now serves so many students (roughly 5 million, about 10–12 percent of the public school population) and consumes a substantial part of education budgets, some people are claiming that too many conditions are considered disabilities and that consequently, many students identified for special education have no "true" disability. So, what is the correct percentage of the school-age population that should be identified as having a disability and needing special education? And how do we know the difference between a "true disability" versus other conditions (e.g., language differences, cultural differences, academic underachievement due to bad teaching, unwillingness to work) that could be effectively addressed or remedied by "non-specialized" education? The answers are, as we have shown in previous chapters, arbitrary. They are arbitrary because the underlying variables determining just who should be identified are continuous distributions—they can vary from a little to a lot, with fine gradations possible. It is a matter of judgment.

Unreliable Identification

Some students have disabilities so significant that nearly everyone recognizes them as "disabilities" immediately or after only a short time. However, the majority of students who have been identified as having a disability or who are likely to be so identified are less clearly, markedly, or unambiguously disabled. They have problems that are better typified as mild than as severe. They are on the margins of disability or, as some have termed it, "judgmentally" disabled.

The criticism that the identification of disabilities is unreliable has significant merit only if you ignore the nature of distributions of human characteristics. As you may recall from earlier discussion, most of the human characteristics that have to do with disabilities are continuously distributed (i.e., they can range from a very little to a lot, with fine gradations possible). For any such distribution the line we draw for classification is arbitrary. Moreover, the closer we draw the line to the average, the more uncertainty we have about individuals who are identified and the larger the number of individuals who are close to the criterion (i.e., who are "borderline"). Thus it is to be expected that identification of students with milder disabilities will be less reliable than identification of those with more severe disabilities. It is *always* judgmental.

Besides, it is important to recognize that uncertainty in identification is not unique to the area of disabilities or to the field of special education. In any area of human function, including medicine, differences of opinion are likely to occur when the condition is "borderline." Some cases (e.g., of cancer or of learning disability) are clear; others are not. Second and third opinions are often sought under such circumstances, and experienced and competent professionals (whether physicians, psychologists, or teachers) may disagree.

Stigmatizes Students and Ruins Identity

Stigma and its opposite, self-esteem, are very important and difficult issues in special education and other social services. We want to shelter people from social stigma whenever possible (i.e., to protect them from social rejection and unfair discrimination because of their differences). We also want to help them develop healthy self-esteem, to see themselves as valuable and capable people who share most of the characteristics of those who are not exceptional. This is particularly difficult when the exceptionality is not giftedness but incompetence at something valued or an inability to perform like most people in a particular part of life.

However, we must also recognize the realities of various types of differences, understand that within any given society *differences differ in their significance*. Some differences are trivial, others tremendously important. But in all societies, the central issue becomes the best way to eliminate stigma and improve self-esteem. Moreover, we need to consider the advisability of eliminating *all* stigma from exceptionality in any society.

Perhaps we should recognize that stigma is a reality in any society and that the skillful and humane management of stigma, not its elimination, is what we should shoot for. In his landmark study of people with mental retardation, anthropologist Robert Edgerton commented on the universality of stigma:

> Both incompetence and stigma management are ubiquitous features of any society, for societies cannot fail to be concerned with the incompetence of their members. Neither can they fail to inflict stigma upon certain, if not all, of their incompetents. Hence, some people in all societies must be both incompetent and stigmatized.[4]

If stigma is ubiquitous or always present in some form in any society, the question becomes how we can best manage or respond to it. Denial that the difference exists (or the pretense that it does not) may allow people to "pass" or to be seen as unexceptional. The gifted person may "pass" as unexceptional in many or most circumstances in which the gift or talent is not featured. The person who cannot perform as expected, and is therefore incompetent in some desired understanding or skill, may be helped to "pass" in many situations. However, what Edgerton described as the "cloak of competence" has substantial limitations in covering or protecting exceptionality. Edgerton described the cloak and the limits of pretense:

> The [formerly institutionalized people with mental retardation] strive to cover themselves with a protective cloak of competence. To their own satisfaction they manage to locate such coverings, but the cloaks that they think protect them are in reality such tattered and transparent garments that they reveal their wearers in all their naked incompetence. In a sense, these retarded persons are like the emperor in the fairy tale who thought he was wearing the most elegant garments but, in fact, was wearing nothing at all.[5]

Providing "cover" and helping someone to "pass" may well be necessary or the most humane thing to do in some circumstances, but such pretense does not address the more fundamental issue of stigma. Empathy, support, accommodation, and acceptance are much more likely to be generated by candid portrayal of a problem, disability, or incompetence.

Writer Martha Randolph Carr described her son Louie's learning disability and her inability to recognize it. She was afraid of labeling her son. Because of her fear, she decided to just read to Louie throughout his elementary school years, as he could not read for himself. Louie's response to his disability finally being labeled when he was in high school was very different from what his mother had anticipated. Instead of being hurt or humiliated, he was relieved and asked, "You mean I'm not stupid?

Were you worried, too?" Ms. Carr realized that her unwillingness to recognize the truth about Louie was the problem, not labeling.[6]

Societal attitudes can change, although such change is often relatively slow and difficult. Consider how social attitudes toward smoking, drunk driving, homosexuality, and cancer have changed over the past several decades. Smoking was once tolerated nearly everywhere, but this is no longer true. Smoking now carries a stigma in many public places. Drunk driving, once tolerated or accepted as a given, is now unacceptable behavior. Homosexuality has emerged from the days of cover-up and shame and is now much more often accepted. Cancer was once a disease to be hidden by those afflicted with it and discussed by those around them in hushed tones. Now cancer is spoken of openly and dealt with as a serious, increasingly treatable and sometimes preventable disease like many others. Perhaps cancer is among the best models for stigma management of disability. The stigma of cancer has abated because people were encouraged to confront it for what it is. It is not nice; it is not desirable; it is not anything we would wish on someone we care about. It is something to be acknowledged and treated. In short, we want people to recognize it for what it is and treat it to minimize its effects. We want people without cancer to take action to prevent it, or at least to reduce the chances of getting it. We want our society to be accepting and supportive of those who have cancer. We could do no better than to work for a similar societal response to disability.

The issue of disability being a stigma was brought home to one of us (Hallahan) recently. He was watching an interview on television of a young mother of a child with Down syndrome. She recounted how she had been terribly offended when after telling someone that she had a Down syndrome child that person had said, "I'm sorry." If she had said her child had cancer, would she have been offended by the same response from the individual? One could, of course, infer that the person saying he was sorry was thinking that the child was somehow less human. And perhaps because of other interactions she had had with people she was quick to infer that that was his intent. But a more literal inference would be that he was sorry because of all the likely hurdles—physical, psychological, and educational—that she and the child would face now and into the future.

In the end, the assumption that special education—the fair, albeit specialized, treatment of exceptionality—*creates* stigma is pernicious. It confuses the treatment with the cause. Would we make the assumption that the treatment of cancer was the cause of the stigma it once carried? Of course not.

Serves Students Too Long

Most of the students who receive special education have *developmental* disabilities. This means that their conditions are usually permanent, not temporary (although they may get better or worse at times) and that there is no known "cure." So the problem is finding the best way of managing the disability, not making it disappear.

Some commentaries reveal a naive view of both special education and the disabilities it addresses. They portray the disability as being more like a broken bone that heals than like diabetes, which is a chronic condition. And they see special education as designed to be more like a cast, which is temporary, than like insulin, which a diabetic will need indefinitely. The conclusion that special education is wasted time and effort because so few students "escape" from it is, in our view, a disgraceful misunderstanding.

The truth is that most students with disabilities will need special teaching, accommodations, or supports throughout school no matter how efficient special education is. And many if not most will require life-long support or special attention if they are to accomplish all they can. The law requires educators and parents to agree that a student no longer needs special education if he or she is to exit special education (i.e., to be "decertified"). The fact that a small percentage of students are dropped or decertified from special education is to be expected, given the nature of developmental disability. The irony is that those who are critical of how long students stay in special education are often the same people who contend that too many students are being misidentified as needing special education.

Should Be Reconceptualized as a Service, Not a Place

This is one of the most curious criticisms of special education because, to our knowledge, special education has been conceptualized by most professionals as a service, not a place, since its origin. We don't know of any special education scholar or leader who has written or conceptualized special education merely as a physical or geographical place, not as a service. So the criticism seems to us to be of the variety many have called a "straw man" or a completely trumped up argument.

Undoubtedly, special education has sometimes been misrepresented as a place, in some cases by the very people who suggest that it be reconceptualized as a service. And sometimes students do not receive or have not received the special instruction that they should in a special school or a special class. This does not mean that special education was wrong in conceptualization; it does mean that it was poorly practiced.

Since its inception, special education has been conceptualized as special instruction. But those who invented special education recognized that special instruction sometimes requires a special place, simply because no teacher is capable of offering all kinds of instruction in the same place and at the same time and that some students need to be taught things that others don't need. So, as has been recognized all along, the specialized places in which special education sometimes occurs are necessary for some special instruction, especially if it is to be done well.

There is no magic in any place, either the regular classroom or a special class. Place, by itself, does not represent good special education. Special education is neither good nor bad because of *where* it is offered. The *instruction* is what matters and what makes special education special. But, as we have suggested in previous chapters, if instruction is actually special, then not everyone gets it. And if it is truly special, then not every teacher can provide it in every context. Sometimes special education demands a special place, but the place does not represent the concept; it does not now, and it never has.

Other Questions About Special Education

Following are some of the additional questions reasonable people might pose about special education. We have attempted to answer these questions previously, but here we reiterate our answers in condensed form.

Who Needs Special Education?

The short answer is that special education is intended to serve those students whose school performance is exceptionally high or low because they have special gifts or talents (in the case of exceptionally high performance) or disabilities (in the case of exceptionally low performance). Another way of putting this is that special education is designed to serve students at the fringes or extremes of distributions of performance if they have a disabling condition or giftedness. Special education is not mandated for gifted students, only for those who have a disability and by reason thereof need special education (see Chapter 3).

Why Do Some Exceptional Students Not Need Special Education?

Some students have disabilities that do not interfere with their school achievement or social adjustment. That is, some students with disabilities do not need special education simply because their educational performance is unaffected. Usually, these are students with physical or sensory disabilities whose academic achievement is unaffected by their disability. Special education is reserved for cases in which the disability affects educational performance, including social development (see Chapter 3).

Why Shouldn't All Students Have Special Education?

Simply put, it is neither reasonable nor feasible to provide special education for every student. *Special* implies something atypical, unusual, and different from the norm. First of all, by definition, not all education can be special education. Second, the extraordinary effort demanded for special education is not reasonable to expect for all students or for all who teach them. The education of all students can be and should be good, but it cannot be *special* for all students (see Chapters 2 and 4).

What Is Special About Special Education?

Special and general education are similar in many respects, often including what is taught and basic instructional procedures. However, special education is more precise, intensive, focused, and relentless than general education. It is different from and more precise on at least the following dimensions: pacing or rate, intensity, relentlessness, structure, reinforcement, pupil:teacher ratio, curriculum, monitoring, and assessment (see Chapter 4). Extraordinary needs demand extraordinary responses. For many exceptional students, full-blown special education—very different education, compared to the typical, even if the typical is good—is required.[7]

What Kinds of Exceptionalities Require Special Education?

For the most part, these exceptionalities include differences in thinking, learning academics, focusing and sustaining attention, controlling emotions and behavior, communicating, hearing, seeing, or some combination of these. Exceptionalities include disabilities and extraordinary abilities that are typically identified as gifts or talents. Some students have both disabilities and special gifts or talents for which special education is needed (see Chapter 3).

Why Do We Need Categories and Labels?

It is impossible to communicate—at least impossible to communicate clearly—without categories and labels. True, categories and labels can be misunderstood or abused, but without them we cannot make sense of human conditions or needs (or, for that matter, anything in the world). It's important not to misinterpret a given label, whatever it may be (e.g., tall, obese, deaf, stutterer, cerebral palsy). We must be on guard against assuming that a label tells us something it does not or reveals everything we need to know about an individual. But without categories and labels we cannot describe people or phenomena. Furthermore, the more specifically and reliably we can label something, the better we can communicate about it. Vague and general labels result in vague and general communication. The problem of stigma is real and important, but stigma is created by social responses to labels or categories, not the labels or categories themselves (see Chapter 3).

What Disabilities Can Be Prevented?

Many disabilities can be prevented by better health care and safety precautions. Many disabilities can be prevented from becoming worse if we identify them early and provide effective treatment. However, some disabilities are going to occur even with our best efforts to prevent them. Human variations and accidents are givens, and we need to be ready to treat and accommodate disabilities regardless of our best preventive efforts (see Chapter 3).

What Do We Know About Prevention?

All of the information we could provide about prevention cannot be provided in our brief answer. We know that the effective *primary* prevention (meaning that the problem never surfaces) of learning and behavior problems requires excellent instruction and behavior management for all students, not just exceptional students. Health care and safety procedures can prevent many disabilities related to diseases, accidents, or physiological problems. Effective *secondary* prevention requires early identification of those students who are beginning to have problems (in learning, behavior, or physical abilities) and special teaching or other intervention to address their problems. Effective secondary prevention either keeps the problem from getting worse or reverses it. *Tertiary* prevention is for cases in which problems are already severe, and it is designed to avoid complications. In all cases and at all levels, good prevention depends on using procedures known to facilitate normal development and minimize problems (see Chapter 3).

Why Can't We Know Exactly Who Needs Special Education and Who Doesn't?

We do know, actually, in some cases, but in many cases we do not and cannot. In many cases, it's a tough call, and people may have serious differences of opinion. This is simply because abilities (and therefore disabilities, too) are related to continuously distributed human characteristics. The point at which we call something a disability or a gift is arbitrary, and the closer to the typical we draw our line the more cases of uncertainty we encounter (see Chapters 2 and 3).

How Would We Know If Special Education Is Effective?

First, let us describe some things that do *not* describe the effectiveness of special education. Special education is *not* more effective because there is more of it. It is *not* more effective because it serves more children. It is *not* effective because it costs more money. It is *not* effective because more students are placed in a given setting (e.g., regular classroom or special school). *Special education is effective if and only if students learn more with it than they would have learned without it.* However, it is very hard, if not impossible, to do scientific experiments to show this, simply because it's not legally or ethically defensible to withhold special education from students for any amount of time just so they can become a scientific "control group." So the best we can do is to look at how students with disabilities or with special gifts fare before they get special education (those with disabilities are all in serious difficulty in school or have obvious disabilities that would prevent them from being typical learners) and then to look at how they do with special education. Special education can't be expected to make students with disabilities just like those without disabilities—to normalize disabilities—but it can improve the quality of life and the academic performance of students over what they would have experienced had they not received special education. Special education is effective to the extent that it provides better instruction than students would receive in general education (see Chapter 4).

Why Can't We Just Leave Special Education up to Local and State Education Agencies?

Perhaps we could do so, but we would then be at considerable risk of losing special education in some localities and states. The federal special education law (IDEA) was passed in response to the failure of localities and states to meet the needs of students with disabilities. It's a matter of balancing the cost of intrusion of federal education policy against the benefit of a uniform policy of meeting the needs of students with disabilities. We feel that the benefit clearly outweighs the cost in this case (see Chapter 1).

Why Does Special Education Cost More Money Than General Education?

A variety of factors runs the cost up, as we discussed earlier and in Chapter 4. Special services (services that not everyone gets) of any kind cost more money than not having them. The primary additional costs of special education have to do with reduced pupil:teacher ratios, special equipment, and transportation (see Chapters 1 and 4).

What Is Inclusion? Is It Always a Bad Idea or Always a Good Idea?

Inclusion is the education of students with disabilities (or giftedness) in the neighborhood schools and classrooms they would attend if they had no exceptionalities. Inclusion is called for in the law (IDEA), but only to the extent that it is feasible and compatible with the best interests of the student. *Full inclusion* refers to placing all exceptional students in regular schools and classes regardless of their characteristics or needs. Full inclusion is illegal, as it ignores the law's demand of a continuum of alternative placement options (CAP), ranging from inclusion in the general education classroom to resource rooms, special classes, special schools, and teaching in the hospital or home, as may be most appropriate for the individual student. The law calls for a case-by-case determination of what is best for the student. For some, inclusion in the general education classroom is, indeed, feasible and appropriate. For other students, however, inclusion is harmful and counterproductive, as they need a more specialized and separate educational setting than can be arranged in a regular classroom if their educational needs are to be met (see Chapters 1 and 4).[8]

Why Is the Full Inclusion of All Students Not Feasible or Desirable?

The full inclusion of all students is not feasible because some require highly specialized and intensive instruction (e.g., in Braille and mobility skills, manual communication, specific academic areas, or social skills). It is not feasible for a regular classroom teacher to teach every possible skill to every possible student and do it well—especially if all the instruction is to occur in the same place and at the same time (see Chapters 3 and 4).

The *full* inclusion of *all* students is not desirable as a policy for several reasons. First, it is illegal. Second, it short-circuits the development of a helpful disability culture. Most of us need some affiliation with others who share our characteristics of religious belief, interests, abilities, disabilities, and so on. Students with disabilities are no exception in this regard. They often find understanding, support, and increased power in congregation. Third, a blanket policy of full inclusion of all students neglects individual differences that are important in academic learning and socialization. As Jean Hall has noted, "By blindly pursuing absolute adherence to a concept, inclusionists have neglected the educational and social needs of individual children."[9]

What Is the Least Restrictive Environment for a Student?

The least restrictive environment (LRE) for a given student is the environment clos-est to the one the student would be in if he or she had no disability, given that the in-structional needs of the student can be met. Federal special education law (IDEA) requires, first, a free appropriate public education (FAPE). After an appropriate edu-cation has been designed for a student, then the education is to be provided in the LRE. For some students, this will be the regular classroom; for others, it will be a more specialized environment, including, for some, a special class or special school (see Chapters 1 and 4).

Who Should Decide Whether a Child Needs Special Education?

This is actually one of special education's perpetual questions—one that isn't going to be answered to everyone's satisfaction because it is a matter of judgment and social convention. The federal law, IDEA, demands that no single individual be allowed to make the decision. The decision is to be made jointly by educators and parents—the people who know the child best and work with him or her the most (see Chapters 2 and 4).

Why Don't We Call Special Education Something Else?

We could, and perhaps we will. We do not think a change in terminology is needed or would improve the education of children with or without disabilities. Changing the label for education designed for exceptional students would not change its nature or substance. Something like "precision teaching" may eventually replace the term "special education," but all of the elements of special education would remain (see Chapters 2 and 4).

Why Not Just Treat Every Child as an Individual?

There are simply not enough resources, and probably there never will be, to have in-dividualized educational planning for all students. Education, like clothes and cars and many other consumer goods, must be designed for the typical if the masses are to receive it. Individualized education for every student is infeasible for the same reasons that tailor-made clothing (as opposed to clothing bought off the rack) for ev-eryone is infeasible. The cost would be prohibitive, and there simply aren't enough and never will be enough personnel to accomplish it (see Chapter 4).

Why Can't All Teachers Be Special Education Teachers?

Being a competent special education teacher takes specialized training—training that isn't feasible or even necessary for all teachers. Just as not all physicians can, or should be, cardiac surgeons, not all teachers can be special educators. It could be argued that the basic training of teachers (or physicians) can be improved, but specialized training—aimed at addressing special conditions and circumstances—always goes beyond basic training. If it does not, then the whole concept of "special" is suspect (see Chapter 4).

What Do We Know About Instructional Approaches That Work Best for Children With Disabilities?

We know that for students who have problems in learning the most effective instructional practices are directive and teacher-controlled. This appears to be true, actually, for all children, even gifted students, not just those with learning problems. Gifted students may learn a lot with little or no direct instruction from a teacher, as they are sometimes self-taught or pick up a lot of information and skills through incidental learning (see Chapter 4).

What Is Wrong With Heterogeneous Grouping for Instruction?

Heterogeneous grouping—grouping together students very different in knowledge of the subject being taught—is going to be boring for those who have already mastered the content and humiliating for those who can't perform adequately. So, it is unsatisfying for the students who are very discrepant from the rest of the group in what they know and are able to do. For the teacher, whether a general or special educator, heterogeneous grouping for instruction presents an insurmountable difficulty. Heterogeneous grouping may be fine for noninstructional activities, but it is good for neither students nor teachers when the focus is on instruction (see Chapters 2 and 4).

What Is Wrong With Homogeneous Grouping for Instruction?

Nothing. Some people have suggested that it is unfair because students are "tracked" or because the lower-performing students get the least competent teachers. However, "tracking" refers to rigid assignment to groups, not the flexible homogeneous grouping for instruction that we recommend. And homogeneous grouping for instruction does not mean that students are homogeneously grouped for every type of school activity (see Chapters 2 and 4).

Why Is There Disproportional Representation of Certain Ethnic Groups and Males in Special Education?

We do not know for certain. The reasons are probably multiple and complex, the same as are the answers to the question about why some students are exceptional. African American students tend to be over-represented in some categories of special education, especially mental retardation and emotional disturbance, but other ethnic groups (e.g., Hispanic and Asian/Pacific Islander students) are often under-represented.[10] Unfair discrimination or racism and sexism might account for some cases. But we cannot ignore the roles of poverty, home experiences, community expectations, genetics, and every other factor known to contribute to the answer to the question of why students have disabilities or are gifted. The more important question for us is whether students who need special education are getting it, regardless of the proportion of any given subpopulation who may be receiving special education (see Chapter 3).

Why Can't Special Education Make Itself Unnecessary Through Effective Prevention and Training?

The fact is that not all cases of disability can be prevented. Even with our best instructional, health, and safety procedures, some individuals will have disabilities and need special education. Moreover, although some special education practices can be implemented by regular classroom teachers in general education, not all of them can be. Nor is being in the regular classroom alongside nonexceptional age peers the best place for all children, regardless of their characteristics and needs. Consequently, special education will always be needed, just as emergency medical care and intensive care units and other specialized services (in medicine, law, or any other profession) will always be needed (see Chapters 2 and 3).

Why Is "Leaving No Child Behind" Impossible?

It would be difficult but possible to achieve good instruction for all children (i.e., "Every child well taught" is within the realm of possibility). However, measurement of anything (achievement included) always produces a distribution of scores, and there is always a "behind" or lower segment in the distribution. Those in the lower range of the distribution can be taught well, but good teaching will not eliminate the lower part of the distribution. Someone is always going to be behind others (see Chapter 2). The second-best is behind the best.

Why Does Good Education Make Kids Less Like Each Other?

Good education is aimed at helping students become even better at what they do well, not just helping those below a standard to reach it. Hence, good education increases the variance and range of the distribution of outcomes. Students learn at different rates, and those who are exceptionally fast inevitably become less like those who are exceptionally slow (or even average) in knowledge and ability in particular areas (see Chapter 2).

Why Can't Everybody Be Average or Better in Something?

The reason is simply because an average is based on a distribution, which always and inevitably has a part below that average. Having everyone or everything above average on any given criterion is a mathematical impossibility. There is also a distribution of how many different things a given person is good at. Some are good at many things, some at few things. Some will be exceptionally good at nothing. Besides, "average" is by definition, a moving target (see Chapter 2).

Where Do Benchmarks or Criteria for Exit, Promotion, or a Diploma Come From?

Benchmarks or other criteria are based on our expectations of what the typical or average student can achieve. The benchmark may be somewhat higher or lower than the current average, but, ultimately, the average (or typical or normal) is what we expect of students or of ourselves. True, the benchmark for being admitted to a given program (e.g., a military academy, gifted program, college, etc.) may be substantially higher than the average. However, the average is always an important reference point in setting a criterion for success or failure (see Chapter 2).

Is Special Education a Legitimate Profession?

Some critics have described special education in very derogatory terms, as wasteful, biased, segregating, ineffective, invalid, and so on.[11] We believe otherwise, as do others, for reasons we have tried to explain here.[12] One of our distinguished colleagues in special education, Hill Walker, made the following comments in accepting the 2003 award for outstanding service from the Midwest Symposium for Leadership in Behavioral Disorders.

> I believe our field stands as a lighthouse beacon of hope, caring and unconditional support for these at-risk children and youth to whom life has dealt such a cruel hand. I have been a researcher in the area of school-related behavior disorders for over three decades. During that time, I have been proud to call myself a member of the field [of emotional and behavioral disorders] which brings together dedicated professionals from diverse backgrounds who work together so well on behalf of at-risk children. Our field models demonstrate positive values and best practices that can make a real difference in the lives of children and youth with emotional and behavioral disorders and those of their families.[13]

Special education stands for the effort to give all students a fair chance to learn academics and social behavior. In our opinion, it is both legitimate and essential to achieve social justice in schooling. Like Walker, we are proud to be associated with the profession of special education, and we believe special educators in every category of exceptionality are doing essential work. Our hope is not merely that special education survives as a profession but that it becomes everything it should be for every exceptional learner.

Summary

Special education is often criticized as follows: It is a failure because it does not produce good outcomes; it costs too much; it serves too many students, including many without disabilities; its identification procedures are unreliable; it stigmatizes students and ruins their identities; it serves students for too many years and does not result in enough students losing their identity as having a disability; and it needs to be reconceptualized as a service, not a place. None of these criticisms is valid. Answering basic questions about special education requires understanding the nature of statistical distributions and the task of teaching.

BOX 5.1

Case in Point

Were the Outcomes Good for Jimmy?

- After one year of special education, Jimmy has increased his reading level from second grade to fourth grade, although he still is not up to the grade level he should be on—Grade 6. He increased his reading level at twice the rate expected for making normal progress through school, but he is still behind his age mates. We think that is very good progress, although it still leaves Jimmy behind most sixth graders. But is he as far behind as he would have been without special education? Probably not. We think he is very, very likely better off than if he had not received special education. So, is the outcome good for him? It all depends on how you look at it.

Did Jimmy's Special Education Cost Too Much?

- It is difficult to calculate the cost of Jimmy's special education for the past year precisely. But the average per pupil cost of education in Jimmy's school district is $9,000 per year, and it appears that the cost for Jimmy was about $12,000 for a year. Was the additional cost too much? We don't think so, but anyone can say they think the cost of education is too high, regardless of what it is. We think the extra cost of $3,000 per year is a bargain, given that Jimmy will likely be much more employable when he finishes school, particularly if his special education continues.

Did Jimmy Unnecessarily Swell the Ranks of Students Getting Special Education?

- That depends on whether you think he needed special education. Was it necessary for him to get it? We think so, but others might argue that he could have "caught up" without special education through more hard work on his part and that of his general education teacher. Would it have been better to identify his reading problem sooner and give him special instruction? Probably so, in our opinion, although the fact that earlier intervention was not provided is not a logical argument that it should not have been provided later. Earlier may be better, but better late than never.

Were the Procedures Used to Identify Jimmy so Unreliable That We Still Don't Really Know Whether He Needed Special Education?

■ The tests given to Jimmy are not perfect, and they have margins of error. However, it does not look to us as if they are grossly inaccurate in assessing Jimmy's performance or in determining appropriate expectations for his learning.

Was Jimmy Stigmatized or Was His Identity Ruined by Receiving Special Education?

■ Some of Jimmy's classmates teased him about his going to special education. Most did not. He was sorry to be identified as failing to meet expectations and receive special education. But he is very happy with his progress. We know that having any problem, regardless of its nature, carries a certain amount of stigma. But we don't see his identity as ruined. Nor do we see the possible stigma as being worse than the frustration, poor self-esteem, and anxiety he might have faced had he been left to fall further and further behind in his reading skills.

Did Jimmy's Special Education "Fail" Because He Still Required Those Special Services After a Year?

■ Jimmy has received special education for one year and has still not reached his grade level in reading. Therefore, his parents and teachers want his special education to continue. He and his parents know that he has a learning disability. Their understanding is that his learning disability is probably going to be present throughout his life. They are not so concerned about his "getting out" of special education as they are about his receiving the special instruction he needs now and for as long as he needs it.

Can the Special Education Jimmy Received Be Best Conceptualized as a Place or as a Service?

■ Jimmy received special instruction. That is a service. It was not feasible for his regular classroom teacher to give him the specialized instruction and extra attention his learning disability required. His special education was not a matter of getting him to a certain location but giving him the instruction he needed. The place he went for that instruction was important only because it allowed the service to be provided most efficiently and effectively.

REFERENCE NOTES

1. Hanushek, Kain, & Rivkin (2002).
2. Helderman (2003, p. B7).
3. Kauffman & Pullen (1996, p. 8). See also Carpenter & Bovair (1996); Kauffman, Bantz, & McCullough (2002).
4. Edgerton (1967, p. 218).
5. Edgerton (1993, p. 193).
6. Carr (2004).
7. See Cook & Schirmer (2003a).

8. For further discussion of inclusion see Gliona, Gonzales, & Jacobson, (2005); Hallahan & Kauffman (2003); Kauffman & Hallahan (1993, 1995, 1997, 2005); Kauffman, Bantz, & McCullough (2002); Mock & Kauffman (2005).

9. Hall (2002, p. 148).

10. National Research Council (2002).

11. For example, Robert Worth (1999), writing in *The Washington Monthly,* said that special education is a scandal that "wastes money and hurts the poor" and that it is "the road to hell." Marc Fisher (2001), writing in *The Washington Post,* said that "Special-ed is the gold-plated garbage can of American schooling." Michelle Cottle (2001), writing in *The New Republic,* describes special education as "a disaster. Poorly defined, poorly run, poorly enforced." Public perceptions of special education and its future have been affected by this barrage of criticism. Writing in *The Journal of Special Education,* Bryan Cook and Barbara Schirmer (2003b) noted the antagonism toward special education: "We were struck by the growing number of disdainful accounts of contemporary special education and found our own perspectives to be quite at odds with what we were reading and hearing" (p. 139). Harsh criticism of special education has also come from special educators and policy makers who state that separate special education does not work or has no advantage for children (e.g., Gartner & Lipsky, 1987, 1989; Reynolds, 1989), compare placement of children outside regular classrooms to slavery and racial discrimination (e.g., Stainback & Stainback, 1991), or portray special education as a failed enterprise that requires radical reform (e.g., the report of the President's Commission on Excellence in Special Education found at the following Website: www.ed.gov/inits/commissionsboards/whspecialeducation/index.html).

12. See Cook & Schirmer (2003b).

13. Walker (2003).

REFERENCES

Bateman, B. D. (1994). Who, how, and where: Special education's issues in perpetuity. *The Journal of Special Education, 27,* 509–520.

Bateman, B. D. (2004). *Elements of successful teaching: General and special education students.* Verona, WI: IEP Resources.

Bateman, B. D., & Linden, M. A. (1998). *Better IEPs: How to develop legally correct and educationally useful programs* (3rd ed.). Longmont, CO: Sopris West.

Berninger, V. W., Abbott, R. D., Vermeulen, K., Ogier, S., Brooksher, R., Zook, D., & Lemos, Z. (2002). Comparison of faster and slower responders to early intervention in reading: Differentiating features of their language profiles. *Learning Disability Quarterly, 25,* 59–76.

Boyda, S. D., Zentall, S. S., & Feiko, D. J. K. (2002). The relationship between teacher practices and the task-appropriate and social behavior of students with behavioral disorders. *Behavioral Disorders, 27,* 236–255.

Carpenter, B., & Bovair, K. (1996). Learning with dignity: Educational opportunities for students with emotional and behavioral difficulties. *Canadian Journal of Special Education, 11*(1), 6–16.

Carr, M. R. (2004, January 4). My son's disability, and my own inability to see it. *Washington Post,* B5.

Cook, B. G., & Schirmer, B. R. (Eds.). (2003a). What is special about special education? [Special issue]. *The Journal of Special Education, 37*(3).

Cook, B. G., & Schirmer, B. R. (2003b). What is special about special education? Introduction to the series. *The Journal of Special Education, 37,* 139.

Cottle, M. (2001, June 18). Jeffords kills special ed. reform school. *The New Republic,* 14–15.

Coyne, M. D., Kameenui, E. J., & Simmons, D. C. (2001). Prevention and intervention in beginning reading: Two complex systems. *Learning Disabilities Research and Practice, 16,* 62–73.

Edgerton, R. B. (1967). *The cloak of competence: Stigma in the lives of the mentally retarded.* Berkeley, CA: University of California Press.

Edgerton, R. B. (1993). *The cloak of competence* (revised and updated) Berkeley, CA: University of California Press.

Engelmann, S. (1997). Theory of mastery and acceleration. In J. W. Lloyd, E. J. Kameenui, & D. Chard (Eds.), *Issues in educating students with disabilities* (pp. 177–195). Mahwah, NJ: Erlbaum.

Espin, C. A., Busch, T. W., Shin, J., & Kruschwitz, R. (2001). Curriculum-based measurement in the content areas: Validity of vocabulary-matching as an indicator of performance in social studies. *Learning Disabilities Research & Practice, 16,* 142–151.

Fisher, M. (2001, December 13). Students still taking the fall for D.C. schools. *The Washington Post,* B1, B4.

Fletcher, J. M., Foorman, B. R., & Boudousquie, A. (2002). Assessment of reading and learning disabilities: A research-based intervention-oriented approach. *Journal of School Psychology, 40,* 27–63.

Foorman, B. R., & Torgesen, J. (2001). Critical elements of classroom and small group instruction to promote reading success in all children. *Learning Disabilities Research and Practice, 16,* 203–212.

Forness, S. R., & Knitzer, J. (1992). A new proposed definition and terminology to replace "serious emotional disturbance" in Individuals with Disabilities Education Act. *School Psychology Review, 21,* 12–20.

Fuchs, D., & Fuchs, L. S. (1994). Inclusive schools movement and the radicalization of special education reform. *Exceptional Children, 60,* 294–309.

Fuchs, D., & Fuchs, L. S. (1995). What's "special" about special education? *Phi Delta Kappan, 76,* 522–530.

Fuchs, L. S., & Fuchs, D. (2001). Principles for the prevention and intervention of mathematics difficulties. *Learning Disabilities Research & Practice, 16,* 85–95.

Gartner, A., & Lipsky, D. K. (1987). Beyond special education: Toward a quality system for all students. *Harvard Educational Review, 57,* 367–395.

Gartner, A., & Lipsky, D. K. (1989). *The yoke of special education: How to break it.* Rochester, NY: National Center on Education and the Economy.

Gliona, M. F., Gonzales, A. K., & Jacobson, E. S. (2005). Suggested changes in thinking about instructional environments and in the language of special education. In J. M. Kauffman & D. P. Hallahan (Eds.), *The illusion of full inclusion: A comprehensive critique of a current special education bandwagon* (2nd ed.). Austin, TX: PRO-ED.

Gould, S. J. (1996a). *Full house: The spread of excellence from Plato to Darwin.* New York: Three Rivers Press.

Gould, S. J. (1996b). *The mismeasure of man* (revised & expanded ed.). New York: Norton.

Gresham, F. M. (2002). Responsiveness to intervention: An alternative approach to the identification of learning disabilities. In R. Bradley, L. Danielson, & D. P. Hallahan (Eds.), *Identification of learning disabilities: Research to practice* (pp. 467–547). Mahwah, NJ: Lawrence Erlbaum Associates.

Hall, J. P. (2002). Narrowing the breach: Can disability culture and full educational inclusion be reconciled? *Journal of Disability Policy Studies, 13,* 144–152.

Hallahan, D. P., & Kauffman, J. M. (2003). *Exceptional learners: Introduction to special education* (9th ed.). Boston: Allyn & Bacon.

Hallahan, D. P., Lloyd, J. W., Kauffman, J. M., Weiss, M., & Martinez, E. (2005). *Learning disabilities: Foundations, characteristics, and effective teaching* (3rd ed.). Boston: Allyn & Bacon.

Hanushek, E. A., Kain, J. F., & Rivkin, S. G. (2002). Inferring program effects for special populations: Does special education raise achievement for students with disabilities? *Review of Economics and Statistics, 84,* 584–599.

Helderman, R. S. (2003, October 6). Va. tries to balance its needs: Budget shortfall threatens to consolidate sister schools for the deaf and blind. *Washington Post,* B1, B7.

Hendrick, I. G., & MacMillan, D. L. (1989). Selecting children for special education in New York City: William Maxwell, Elizabeth Farrell, and the development of ungraded classes, 1900–1920. *The Journal of Special Education, 22,* 395–417.

Heward, W. L. (2003). Ten faulty notions about teaching and learning that hinder the effectiveness of special education. *The Journal of Special Education, 36,* 186–205.

Hirsch, E. D., Jr. (1987). *Cultural literacy: What every American needs to know.* New York: Random House.

Hirsch, E. D., Jr. (1996). *The schools we need and why we don't have them.* New York: Anchor.

Horner, R. H., Sugai, G., & Horner, H. F. (2000). A schoolwide approach to student discipline. *School Administrator, 57,* 20–23.

Horner, R. H., Sugai, G., Todd, A. W., Lewis-Palmer, T. (1999–2000). Elements of behavior support plans: A technical brief. *Exceptionality, 8,* 205–215.

Huefner, D. S. (2000). *Getting comfortable with special education law: A framework for working with children with disabilities.* Norwood, MA: Christopher-Gordon.

Huitt, W. G., & Vessel, G. G. (2003). Character development. In J. W. Guthrie (Ed.), *Encyclopedia of education* (2nd ed). New York: Macmillan Reference USA.

Kauffman, J. M. (1981). Introduction: Historical trends and contemporary issues in special education in the United States. In J. M. Kauffman & D. P. Hallahan (Eds.), *Handbook of special education* (pp. 3–23). Englewood Cliffs, NJ: Prentice-Hall.

Kauffman, J. M. (1999). How we prevent the prevention of emotional and behavioral disorders. *Exceptional Children, 65,* 448–468.

Kauffman, J. M. (2002). *Education deform: Bright people sometimes say stupid things about education.* Lanham, MD: Scarecrow Education.

Kauffman, J. M. (2003). Appearances, stigma, and prevention. *Remedial and Special Education, 24,* 195–198.

Kauffman, J. M. (2004). Foreword for H. M. Walker, E. Ramsey, & F. M. Gresham, *Antisocial behavior in school: Strategies and best practices* (2nd ed., pp. xix–xxi). Belmont, CA: Wadsworth.

Kauffman, J. M. (2005a). *Characteristics of emotional and behavioral disorders of children and youth* (8th ed.). Upper Saddle River, NJ: Prentice-Hall.

Kauffman, J. M. (2005b). How we prevent the prevention of emotional and behavioral difficulties in education. In P. Clough, P. Garner, J. T. Pardeck, & F. K. O. Yuen (Eds.), *Handbook of emotional and behavioral difficulties in education* (pp. 366–376). London: Sage Publications.

Kauffman, J. M. (in press a). Waving to Ray Charles: Missing the meaning of disability. *Phi Delta Kappan.*

Kauffman, J. M. (in press b). The president's commission and the devaluation of special education. *Education and Treatment of Children.*

Kauffman, J. M., Bantz, J., & McCullough, J. (2002). Separate and better: A special public school class for students with emotional and behavioral disorders. *Exceptionality, 10,* 149–170.

Kauffman, J. M., & Hallahan, D. P. (1993). Toward a comprehensive delivery system for special education. In J. I. Goodlad & T. C. Lovitt (Eds.), *Integrating general and special education* (pp. 73–102). Columbus, OH: Merrill/Macmillan.

Kauffman, J. M., & Hallahan, D. P. (Eds.). (1995, 2005). *The illusion of full inclusion: A comprehensive critique of a current special education bandwagon.* Austin, TX: Pro-Ed.

Kauffman, J. M., & Hallahan, D. P. (1997). A diversity of restrictive environments: Placement as a problem of social ecology. In J. W. Lloyd, E. J. Kameenui, & D. Chard (Eds.), *Issues in educating students with disabilities* (pp. 325–342). Hillsdale, NJ: Erlbaum.

Kauffman, J. M., & Landrum, T. J. (in press). *Children and youth with emotional and behavioral disorders: A brief history of their education.* Austin, TX: Pro-Ed.

Kauffman, J. M., Mostert, M. P., Trent, S. C., & Hallahan, D. P. (2002). *Managing classroom behavior: A reflective case-based approach* (3rd ed.). Boston: Allyn & Bacon.

Kauffman, J. M., & Pullen, P. L. (1996). Eight myths about special education. *Focus on Exceptional Children, 28*(5), 1012.

Kavale, K. A. (2002). Discrepancy models in the identification of learning disability. In R. Bradley, L. Danielson, & D. P. Hallahan (Eds.), *Identification of learning disabilities: Research to practice* (pp. 369–426). Mahwah, NJ: Lawrence Erlbaum Associates.

Kavale, K. A., & Forness, S. R. (2000a). History, rhetoric, and reality: Analysis of the inclusion debate. *Remedial and Special Education, 21,* 279–296.

Kavale, K. A., & Forness, S. R. (2000b). Policy decisions in special education: The role of meta-analysis. In R. Gersten, E. P. Schiller, & S. Vaughn (Eds.), *Contemporary special education research: Syntheses of the knowledge base on critical instructional issues* (pp. 281–326). Mahwah, NJ: Lawrence Erlbaum.

Kohn, A. (1999). *The schools our children deserve: Moving beyond traditional classrooms and "tougher standards."* Boston: Houghton Mifflin.

Lewis, T. J., Colvin, G., & Sugai, G. (2000). The effects of pre-correction and active supervision on the recess behavior of elementary students. *Education & Treatment of Children, 23,* 109–121.

MacMillan, D. L., & Hendrick, I. G. (1993). Evolution and legacies. In J. I. Goodlad & T. C. Lovitt (Eds.), *Integrating general and special education.* Columbus, OH: Merrill/Macmillan.

Mann, L. (1979). On the trail of process: A historical perspective on cognitive processes and their training. New York: Grune & Stratton.

Mock, D. R., & Kauffman, J. M. (2005). The delusion of full inclusion. In J. W. Jacobson, J. A. Mulick, & R. M. Foxx (Eds.), *Fads: Dubious and improbable treatments for developmental disabilities* (pp. 113–128). Mahwah, NJ: Erlbaum.

Moody, S. W., Vaughn, S., Hughes, M. T., & Fischer, M. (2000). Reading instruction in the resource room: Set up for failure. *Exceptional Children, 66,* 305–316.

National Research Council (2002). *Minority students in special and gifted education.* Committee on Minority Representation in Special Education. M. S. Donovan & C. T. Cross (Eds.). Division of Behavioral and Social Sciences Education. Washington, DC: National Academy Press.

Popham, J. W. (2000). *Modern educational measurement: Practical guides for educational leaders* (3rd ed.). Boston: Allyn & Bacon.

Popham, J. W. (2002). *Classroom assessment: What teachers need to know* (3rd ed.). Boston: Allyn & Bacon.

Presidents Commission on Excellence in Special Education. (2002). *A New Era: Revitalizing Special Education for Children and their Families.* Available at *www.ed.gov/inits/commissionsboards/whspecialeducation/index.html.* Washington, DC: U.S. Department of Education.

Rashotte, C. A., MacPhee, K. & Torgesen, J. K. (2001). The effectiveness of a group reading instruction program with poor readers in multiple grades. *Learning Disability Quarterly, 24,* 119–134.

Ravitch, D. (2003). *The language police: How pressure groups restrict what students learn.* New York: Knopf.

Reynolds, M. C. (1989). An historical perspective: The delivery of special education to mildly disabled and at-risk students. *Remedial and Special Education, 10*(6), 7–11.

Sarason, S. B., & Doris, J. (1979). *Educational handicap, public policy, and social history.* New York: Macmillan.

Sasso, G. M. (2001). The retreat from inquiry and knowledge in special education. *The Journal of Special Education, 34,* 178–193.

Shores, R. E, & Wehby, J. H. (1999). Analyzing the classroom social behavior of students with EBD. *Journal of Emotional & Behavioral Disorders, 7,* 194–199.

Singer, J. D. (1988). Should special education merge with regular education? *Educational Policy, 2,* 409–424.

Stainback, W., & Stainback, S. (1984). A rationale for the merger of special and regular education. *Exceptional Children, 51,* 102–111.

Stainback, W., & Stainback, S. (1991). A rational for integration and restructuring: A synopsis. In J. W. Lloyd, N. N. Singh, & A. C. Repp (Eds.), *The regular education initiative: Alternative perspectives on concepts, issues, and models* (pp. 225–239). Sycamore, IL: Sycamore.

Sutherland, K. S., Wehby, J. H., & Yoder, P. J. (2002). Examination of the relationship between teacher praise and opportunities for students with EBD to respond to academic requests. *Journal of Emotional & Behavioral Disorders, 10,* 5–13.

Swanson, H. L., & Hoskyn, M. (2001). Instructing adolescents with learning disabilities: A component and composite analysis. *Learning Disabilities Research and Practice, 16,* 109–119.

Troia, G. A., & Graham, S. (2002). The effectiveness of a highly explicit, teacher directed strategy instruction routine: Changing the writing performance of students with learning disabilities. *Journal of Learning Disabilities, 35,* 290–305.

U.S. Department of Education. (2002). *Twenty-fourth annual report to Congress on implementation of the Individuals with Disabilities Education Act.* Washington, DC: Author.

Vaughn, S., & Fuchs, L. S. (Eds.). (2003). Redefining learning disabilities as inadequate response to instruction. *Learning Disabilities Research and Practice, 18*(3) [special issue].

Vaughn, S., Gersten, R., & Chard, D. J. (2000). The underlying message in LD intervention research: Findings from research syntheses. *Exceptional Children, 67,* 99–114.

Vaughn, S., Linan-Thompson, S., Kouzekanani, K., Bryant, D. P., Dickson, S., & Blozis, S. A. (2003). Reading instruction grouping for students with reading difficulties. *Remedial and Special Education, 24,* 301–315.

Walker, H. M. (2003, February 20). *Comments on accepting the Outstanding Leadership Award from the Midwest Symposium for Leadership in Behavior Disorders.* Kansas City, KS: Author.

Walker, H. M., & Sprague, J. R. (1999). Longitudinal research and functional behavioral assessment issues. *Behavioral Disorders, 24,* 335–337.

Will, M. C. (1986). Educating children with learning problems: A shared responsibility. *Exceptional Children, 52,* 411–415.

Worth, R. (1999). The scandal of special-ed: It wastes money and hurts the poor. *The Washington Monthly, 31*(6).

Yell, M. L. (1998). *The law and special education.* Upper Saddle River, NJ: Prentice-Hall.

Zigmond, N. (1997). Educating students with disabilities: The future of special education. In J. W. Lloyd, E. J. Kameenui, & D. Chard (Eds.), *Issues in educating students with disabilities* (pp. 377–390). Mahwah, NJ: Erlbaum.

Zigmond, N. (2003). Where should students with disabilities receive special education services? Is one place better than another? *The Journal of Special Education, 37,* 193–199.

INDEX

ARC, 4, 11

Assessment (*see also* Measurement), 48, 53

Attention deficit-hyperactivity disorder (ADHD), 34–35

    definition of, 34–35

    special education and, 35

Autism (*see* Autistic spectrum disorder)

Autistic spectrum disorder, 40

    definition of, 40

    special education and, 40

Average (*see also* Central tendency), 18–20, 23, 71

Benchmarks in assessment, 22, 71

Blindness, 38–39

    definition of, 38–39

    special education and, 39

Brown v. Board of Education of Topeka, 5

Bureau of Education for the Handicapped (BEH), 5

CAP (*see* Continuum of alternative placements)

CEC (*see* Council for Exceptional Children)

Central tendency, 18–19

Communication disorder, 36–37

    definition of, 36–37

    special education and, 37

Contemporary issues, 7

Continuum of alternative placements (CAP), 6–7, 29, 67

Council for Exceptional Children (CEC), 4

Criterion-referenced testing (*see* Benchmarks in assessment)

Curriculum, 8, 9, 29, 48, 52

Deafness, 37–38

    definition of, 37

    special education and, 38

Deaf-blindness and other severe and multiple disabilities, 41–42

    definition of, 41–42

    special education and, 42

Dilemmas in special education, 8–9

Disability and inability, 30

Disproportional representation in special education, 2, 69–70

Education of All Handicapped Children Act (EAHCA; *see also* IDEA), 5

Educational disabilities, 28–46

    continuous distributions and, 31

    inability and, 30

    mild, 31

Emotional or Behavioral Disorder (EBD), 35–36

    definition of, 35–36

    internalizing and externalizing behavior, 36

    special education and, 36

English as a Second Language (ESL), 4

English Language Learners (ELL), 4

Exceptionality, 29–30

    educational defined, 29–30

    characteristics and, 29–30

Facts about special education, 2–3

FAPE (*see* Free, appropriate public education)

Free, appropriate public education (FAPE), 6–7

Full inclusion (*see* Inclusion)

Full inclusion movement (FIM; *see* Inclusion)

General education, 8, 9, 10, 13, 25, 29, 33–35, 43, 47–55, 59, 64, 66–67, 70

General education curriculum, 8, 9, 29, 52

Giftedness and special talents, 42–43

    definition of, 42

    special education and, 43

Heterogeneous grouping, 69

Heterogeniety, 25, 70

History of special education, 3–7

Homogeneous grouping, 69

IDEA (*see* Individuals with Disabilities Education Act)

IEP (*see* Individualized education program)

Inclusion, 6, 7, 8, 10, 29, 54, 67
    advantages and disadvantages, 54, 67
    and law, 7
    definition, 7, 67

Individuals with Disabilities Education Act (IDEA), 6–7, 10, 28, 40, 53, 54, 59

Individualized education program (IEP), 6–7, 53

Individuals with Disabilities Education Act (*see* IDEA)

Intensity of instruction, 48, 49

IQ (*see* Intelligence)

Intelligence
    measurement of, 17, 24
    mental retardation and, 31–32

Labeling, 43–44, 59, 61–62, 65

Learning disability (LD), 33–34
    definition of, 33–34
    special education and, 34

Least restrictive environment (LRE), 6–7, 68

LRE (*see* Least restrictive environment)

Mean (*see* Central tendency)

Measurement (*see* also Statistical distribution), 12–27
    accuracy of, 16–18
    changes in due to special education, 24–26
    meaning of individual score, 23–24
    mistakes in, 9
    problems in, 12–18
    tools for, 15–16
    uncertainty about, 22, 23, 44
    what to measure, 11–15

Median (*see* Central tendency)

Mental retardation (MR), 31–33
    definition of, 31–32
    degrees of, 32
    special education and, 33

Misconceptions, 1–3

Mode (*see* Central tendency)

Monitoring (*see* also Assessment)

Multiple disabilities (*see* Deaf-blindness), 41–42

Need for special education, 28–43
    attention deficit-hyperactivity disorder and, 35
    autistic spectrum disorder and, 40
    blindness and, 39
    communication disorder and, 37
    continuous distributions and, 31
    deafness and, 38
    deaf-blindness, severe, and multiple disabilities and, 42
    exceptionality and, 64–65
    emotional or behavioral disorder and, 36
    giftedness and special talents and, 43
    IDEA and, 28
    learning disability and, 34
    mental retardation and, 33
    physical disability and, 39–40
    traumatic brain injury and, 41
    types of exceptionality and, 29–30
    when not needed for students with disabilities, 43, 64

No child left behind, impossibility of, 70

Office of Special Education Programs (OSEP), 5

Pacing of instruction, 48, 49

Perpetual issues, 7

Physical disability, 39–40
    definition of, 39
    special education and, 39–40

Placement (*see* also Inclusion), 6–8, 29, 52, 54, 63, 67

Public Law 94-142 (*see* Individuals with Disabilities Education Act)

President's Commission on Excellence in Special Education (PCESE), 27, 74

Prevention of disabilities, 23, 43–45, 65–66
    primary, 43
    requirements for, 23
    secondary, 43
    tertiary, 43–44
    why not practiced, 43–45

Pupil:teacher ratio, 48, 52, 55, 56, 59, 64, 67

Rate of instruction (*see* Pacing)
Regular education initiative (REI), 7
Reinforcement, 48, 51
Relentlessness of instruction, 50

Severe disability (*see* Deaf-blindness)
Special education
    as local and state responsibility, 66
    bottom line of, 54–55
    compared to general education, 1, 47–53,
        55, 59, 64, 66, 67
    contemporary and perpetual issues in, 7
    continuum of, 53–54
    cost and, 59, 67
    criticisms of, 57–63
    curriculum and, 52
    defined, 47–48, 64
    effectiveness of, 25–26, 58, 66
    exit from, 62–63
    for everyone, 64
    history of, 3–7
    identification for, 8, 60, 66
    individualization and, 6–9, 47–55, 67–68
    instruction that works and, 69
    intensity and, 49–50
    legitimacy of, 71
    made unnecessary, impossibility of, 70
    misconceptions and facts about, 1–3
    monitoring or assessment and, 53
    nature of, 47–56

number served and, 59–60
outcomes of, 57–59
pacing or rate of instruction and, 49
place versus service, 63
pupil:teacher ratio and, 52
puzzle of, 1, 8–10
questions about, 64–71
reinforcement and, 51–52
relentlessness and, 50
stigma and, 8, 11, 57, 60–62, 65
structure and, 51
Statistical distribution
    changes in produced by special education,
        24–26
    continuous, 20, 31
    definition, 18–20
    discrete categories and, 21, 22
    importance of, 20–21
    individual scores in, 22–23
Stigma, 8, 11, 57, 60–62, 65
Structure, 48, 51

Talented (*see* Giftedness and special talents)
Teacher training, 8–9
Traumatic brain injury (TBI), 40–41
    definition of, 40–41
    special education and, 41

Vision impairment (*see* Blindness)